# My Journey to Endor

A True Story by Kevin Thompson
About my journey making the Star Wars Saga
"Return of the Jedi"

Written by
## Tracey McCoy Thompson

To our son Wyatt.

*To be Jedi is to face the truth, and choose.*
*Give off light, or darkness, Padawan.*
*Be a candle or the night. ~ Yoda*

You are our candle.

## From the Desk of Albin Johnson
*TK210, Legion Founder*
*Fighting 501st Legion Star Wars Costuming Fan Club*
*Carolina Garrison*
www.501st.com
*www.albinjohnson.com*

The "hero's journey" is a concept a lot of us were first introduced to thanks to Star Wars. It describes the path of a young hero as he or she travels far from home, overcomes adversity, and comes back a changed person. The older I get, the more I've come to realize just how many hero's journeys are being told in the Saga. From the redemption of Anakin to the bystander's view of Artoo, adventures are best enjoyed when you see them from different perspectives.

Now imagine my plight: twenty five-years building a Legion of Stormtroopers, only to learn the story of a single Ewok (you know, the ones who kicked our butts on Endor?) turns out to be one of the best hero's journeys of all. But that's Kevin for you. His story is so relatable, you'd almost think he was describing your childhood, your first job interview, and your first big chance to shine. But he did it on the biggest stage imaginable and in an industry that eats heroes for breakfast.

Anyone who's met Kevin knows he and his wife Tracey are always the bright spot of the Star Wars scene. They are tireless in their enthusiasm. They make every fan feel like part of the family. Kevin has without a doubt braved the rigors of the entertainment machine, accomplished things others thought impossible, inspired others with his deeds, and won the race (and the girl!). And he did it all with the courage of a hero.

Now that's a story worth telling.


- Albin Johnson
  Founder, 501st Legion Stormtroopers

# Contents

Dear Reader,

I want to take you on my incredible journey as an Ewok in the film, *Return of the Jedi*. I promise to bring you along on the entire trip and all its ups and downs. My experience at 22 years old molded my life in a universal way and I'm excited to relive it as I share it with you.

Before we start, I want to let you know I am grateful for my time as an actor and stuntman. If I were starting out today, I simply wouldn't have the career I had. The Ewoks and many other costumed characters I played have become extinct. As the television and film industry changes, careers change along with it. With the latest technology, the industry has made puppets, costume characters, special effects, live animals, and locations computer-generated images (CGI).

I don't think most people are aware of it, but the industry has used CGI to make average size actors appear to be dwarfs. The films, *The Hobbit* and *The Lord of the Rings* used this technology. I can't help but think of the shameful piece of entertainment history when white actors put on black faces. It surprises me that something like this is happening today. I'm so happy to hear about work being done to diversify Hollywood and bring populations of underrepresented people into the fold, but I'm shocked and saddened to find that Little People actors don't seem to be part of that trend.

I know we have work to do to try and change the industry for Little People actors. And it's not just about CGI taking jobs away. Why don't we see Little People in mainstream films and television shows, playing fathers, mothers, best friends, teachers, doctors, janitors, or chefs? We live in the world in these roles in real life. Why aren't we cast in them in the industry?

With that, let's climb into our time machine and go back to when big, bulky, furry costumes could be worn by a little person stunt actor pretending to be a fantastic creature called an "Ewok." Where we were dirty, sweaty, and mostly blind as we ran over gargantuan logs, swung from vines, leapt from the highest treetops, and battled the Dark Side. Join me. Let's go to the Forest Moon of Endor.

# Prologue

I SAT IN THE back of the jeep as it rambled through the forest. My body, covered in fur, was sweaty, but I had gotten used to it. With my Ewok head off I could feel the cool, crisp air on my face. I savored it. As the jeep crested a bluff, the set up for my next stunt came into view: a seventy-foot crane on the edge of a cliff.

The cameramen from Industrial Light and Magic (ILM), George Lucas' special effects team, shared the plan. With the help of the crane and a harness, I would swing across a wide valley. Thanks to special effects, it would ultimately look like I landed on a platform in the Ewok Village.

The scene was where the Ewoks capture the heroes and carry them on long poles, like barbequed pigs on a spit at a hula party. I would wave to my Ewok family, and swing into the village.

I was told the crane operator was the best in the county. This took my nerves down a little until I thought about it. *How many crane operators were there in this small county?* It felt like we were in the middle of nowhere. I tried to push the distracting thought away.

The prop guys attached a sandbag to the crane for a test run. The bag, standing in for me, took the flight I would travel. The distance seemed endless as the sandbag floated across the valley. When it finally reached the end of its pendulum swing, my stunt buddy told me that was where I would pretend to land. I'd put my feet down to make it look like I landed on an imaginary platform. It would be drawn into place in post-production.

I watched the sandbag. The first part of the swing looked good and I was feeling confident until… on the return, it was impaled by a sharp wooden post! The bag hung there, like a dead animal. More distracting thoughts flooded in…. *That could be me. What if the cable snapped? What if I fell? Would I die slowly? Would I not feel a thing?*

As the crane operator made adjustments, my stunt buddy came over and put his arm around me. We went over the actions and he reminded me to keep the swing steady all the way through. It was important that I didn't struggle or wiggle. Nice and easy swing out. Nice and easy swing back.

I stared down at the creepy sight below—an orchard of dead trees. Leafless and black they twisted, reaching up like prickly hands from the underworld waiting for their next catch. *Definitely don't want to fall and land on those*, I thought.

I kissed the fresh air goodbye as my wardrobe gal put my head on, and soon I was standing in full costume, alone. Suddenly, a gust of wind whipped by, almost knocking me off my mark. *That would have been great.* I imagined the headline, "Ewok Stuntman Falls to Death Seconds Before Performing Stunt!" I had to shake it off. I took a deep breath, adjusted my footing, and focused. I had to stay balanced as I waited for the director to shout that magic word, "Action."

Was I ready?

Of course I was. I had been preparing for this since I was a kid.

# Chapter One
## Hyper Kid, Hyper Drive

Up, high in the forest that day, I was an Ewok about to swing into the village. I could see C3PO, R2D2, Han Solo, and Chewy below, but I could also see what wasn't there - the village, the platform. I could see, vividly, what ILM would later add with movie magic. Even though I was twenty-two years old, I felt like a kid again, playing in my backyard.

Most kids play make-believe. At least I hope they still do. I did it all the time. I fought dragons, black knights, and took on huge armies. My house and the others on our cul de sac melted away and my imagination whisked me off to mountaintops, beaches, and jungles. The four giant California Oak trees . . . the bamboo forest lining the back wall of the yard . . . the plethora of different bushes and small trees . . . all became enemies, hiding places, and mythical creatures.

My mother would often yell out the window, "Don't smash the flowers!"

She loved her azaleas. I did not love her azaleas. They always stuck to my clothes when I hid under them. My mom knew exactly where I had been when it was dinnertime because the little bright pink tattle-tales were stuck to my shirt!

Our home was built in the 1920s and sat on an oversized lot, perfect for my wild imagination. The two-story house was white with green

1

trim and had a wrap-around veranda with an outside staircase leading up to it. One of the best things about the veranda was that it served as a secret passageway to the roof. With a little balance and grace, I could pull myself up and into another realm. On top of the house, off of my mother's radar, I was free to do as I pleased. I felt like a giant, hiding up in the clouds, quietly looking down on everything below.

The old sturdy brick wall bordering our neighbor's yards was perfect for walking on, crawling beside, falling off, and clamoring back up on. Vegetation covered the path of the wall. I would crawl along until I could not see one foot in front of me. My imagination would go into hyper drive—*who was hiding in the nearby trees? What was readying an attack from the shrubs?* My playmates, which often times were my brothers, would be my allies. And if we all wanted to be the Army General, we'd be on opposing sides. Enemies!

I learned how to do dramatic death scenes when shot by pretend bullets. Falling from the wall was dangerous so we had to train ourselves to do it without getting hurt. I practiced falling from everywhere without getting injured—including the veranda staircase. My mom quickly realized I would bounce up, just like a rubber ball.

Our old green swing set was another vehicle of imagination. My dad bought it second hand and it was made of heavy-duty metal, so strong that a grown man could go for a swing. But to me, it wasn't just an old swing set. It was a rocketship! It was an airplane! It was my own personal flying fantastical beast! That swing set was anything and everything, depending on my mood and chosen game. But one thing was always the same—I constantly fell off it. Countless times. Though I did ring my bell (head) more than once, I never broke any bones. I was always getting stitched up. Thanks to me, my parents were on a first name basis with the emergency room doctors.

In my own personal world, everyone was in on the games. The family dog, Duke, a large German shepherd, played the part of a good wolf. He protected us from our enemies and sometimes took off to chase enemies of his own. One day he jumped off the veranda to chase the mailman! After that, we didn't get our mail for a week. We remedied the situation by putting chicken wire on top of the veranda.

It worked to keep Duke out of trouble but added a new challenge to my now-not-so-secret trips to the roof. My mom always knew by the telltale sign of the bent chicken wire . . . . The jig was up!

From dawn to dusk we would play outdoors, taking snack breaks in between our imaginary adventures, and if we were lucky, we could play at night . . . even when the streetlights came on. By the end of the day, we were covered in dirt, twigs, scrapes, and bruises. And I loved it.

Little did I know back then; my make-believe world would become my profession.

# Chapter Two
# Built in Trademark

AT EIGHT-YEARS-OLD, I was a little shorter than my friends . . . they were getting the growth spurts and I wasn't. That's when I found out that I was a Little Person—a person with short stature, or some people preferred to call me a Dwarf. To me, I was just short! My friends and family, however, were all average size.

My father owned a Neighborhood Pharmacy in the Greater Los Angeles area. My favorite thing about the store was its gigantic display of candy. It was every kid's dream! With a family of eight, school, church, sports, Cub Scouts, and other extracurricular activities, we had a lot of friends. I felt like everyone knew me—because they did! My dwarfism was my built-in trademark.

My mom would say, "Smile to everyone because they will remember you." I wondered, *how in the begeezers would they remember me?* It must be that built-in trademark I was born with. They knew me even if I didn't recognize them.

My trademark did more than get me recognized—it got me a swimming pool. My dad was told that swimming was the best exercise for Little People because it wasn't too hard on the joints and back. He also thought that having a pool would put me at the same advantage as my "average size" siblings and friends. In the water, I was the same size as everyone else. Of course, my siblings were quick to agree. "Yes, definitely, Dad. We need a pool—for Kevin!"

It took me awhile to learn to swim. At first, I sank like a rock. My mom took me to swimming lessons and once the pool was in, I was ready to go. I graduated and was swimming like a fish. Regardless of the weather (swimming in fifty-degree weather is completely fine!) my parents would have to coax me out of that water.

The pool was large and had a diving board. My brothers and I had a new way to use our imagination. We flipped, twisted, and jumped all day long. When my parents weren't home, we leapt off the roof into the pool! There was no fear—it was all about adventure and fun. When I think about it now, as a father myself, I feel lucky to have survived some of those childhood stunts.

When I wasn't playing outside or swimming, I was watching *Billy Barty's Big Top*. Billy was a variety show actor who stood only 3'9" tall—a dwarf who pioneered equality for Little People. He was athletic, like me, and started both a baseball and basketball team made up entirely of Little People athletes and comedians called, *The Hollywood Shorties*. They were the shortest professional sports team in the world.

I was eleven when my mother brought me to a *Shorties* baseball game in 1971. I sat and watched in awe . . . the players—all my size—were funny, entertaining, *and* they were good athletes. After the game, my mother introduced herself to the team. She boasted about me like any mother would, even telling them I was the next Joe DiMaggio. They smiled and signed me up. The very next day I was in the game! I had a new agent. My mother! And I loved her for it!

I continued on the team for the next thirty years, traveling around the world. The experience was incredible. It taught me how to get up in front of people and perform, but later grew into something even bigger.

The team was about more than sports and entertainment—we were about helping others. We raised money for schools and helped support our Little People community, assisting with medical costs and adoption fees. Little People have medical needs and sometimes require surgeries. Many times, dwarfism is considered a pre-existing condition and surgeries may not be covered by health insurance. Little People sometimes have difficulty carrying a full-term child, and for those wanting to start a family, adoption costs can be prohibitive. We aimed to help those in need.

Our charity work planted a seed that grew into a lifetime of fundraising, advocating, and educating. My wife and I continue to find joy in giving back to the community. It's an important part of who we are.

# Chapter Three
# Athletic Theatre Geek

IN HIGH SCHOOL, I prolonged my make-believe world by joining the theatre department. I stayed active, competing in gymnastics and wrestling. I was an athletic theatre geek!

I am extremely compact, so I was able to do very muscular gymnastic moves easier than my teammates. I tried all the events but my size limited me to floor exercise, rings, and parallel bars. I stayed with my personal strengths and focused on the parallel bars.

I designed my routine for my own uniqueness, adapting moves to better suit me. Because of my small hands, many of the tricks were swinging moves. In the beginning, I would often lose my grip and fall. Thank goodness I knew how to land—it must have been that veranda. I was amazed I didn't break my neck, and so was my coach.

My teammates said my routine pumped them up and helped them perform their best. And maybe they were right—we were league champs my senior year!

As much as I loved gymnastics, I never planned on wrestling. But the team needed someone in my weight class. Ninety-eight-pound wrestlers are not easy to find.

I had no idea about the moves, leverage, or physics of wrestling. I was recruited on a Thursday and we had a tournament that Saturday. I went to my first practice and sweated more than I ever had before.

We ran laps around the field and up and down the bleachers. Then we broke into groups according to our weight. I wrestled kids that were heavier than me because there wasn't anyone close to my weight. I had no idea what I was doing. The guys helped me along, but never let me win. That practice was the toughest thing I had ever done. I went home and died!

The next day, practice was more of the same but I started getting the hang of it. I studied the other wrestlers as they competed and noticed some were strong, others were fast; each wrestler used their strengths. I had strength and wits. Wait, did I have my wits? Yeah, I did.

On the day of the tournament, the coach handed me a uniform that reminded me of those old-time photos of the strong man with the handlebar mustache. It was one piece and it was tight. I even looked like a strong man because it pulled everything in. Shortly after weighing in, (ninety-two pounds) I found out why the coach *really* wanted me on the team: If the other team didn't have someone in my weight class, they forfeited that match. I'd win without actually competing! What luck! This was great news, but my luck didn't last.

In my next match, I went up against the state champion. He had pinned his last ten opponents. And though he didn't manage to pin me, he wiped the mat with me. I was so tired I could barely move.

As much as I enjoyed playing sports, the theatre department beckoned. But there was one teeny tiny problem: due to its popularity (it had a reputation of being one of the best in the San Gabriel Valley), it was not available for freshman and sophomores. I wanted to join in the fun so badly that I attempted to get in my sophomore year anyway. I turned on the charm and tried to convince Mr. Reed, the department head, to let me in.

He didn't. I don't want to say I didn't have any charm. I think he had heard that song and dance before. He was the drama teacher. He taught song and dance. I only had gymnastics and wrestling moves. I would have to wait a little longer to test my acting chops.

When my junior year finally rolled around, I got into drama *and* television production. This was a homerun! I could perform with drama and make movies with TV production. It was like playing in my backyard again and I loved it!

In TV production we wrote and produced our own films. Our teacher read the scripts and asked how we would tackle shooting. He would accept, reject, or help modify our ideas. It was just like the real world. After the films were done, we sold tickets for a film festival.

When my films were shown, everyone knew they were mine. They had a unique look. When shooting, I put the camera on a tripod to get a steady shot. I filmed what I saw at my eye level so it was literally, my vision. My trademark seemed to come out in everything I did.

My experience with theatre and film had a huge influence on my life. The theatre department was especially impactful. Mr. Reed told me to use my size as an asset rather than a hindrance. His words resonated with me and really stuck, helping to shape the way I presented myself to the world. Gymnastics, wrestling, making films, and the opportunities with the theatre department put me out in front. And thanks to Mr. Reed's advice, I was ready.

Every year our high school had a big talent show. A host would welcome the audience and chat between acts. Usually it was one of the most distinguished seniors from the theatre department. Even though I hadn't been in any high school productions yet, they picked me--a junior. I was excited and nervous.

The director wanted me to have my own segment, so we wrote a script about "my trademark" and what it was like being a Little Person. I spoke about how people treated me because I looked a little different. But we all look different—that's what makes us who we are. As I wrapped up the segment with my closing words, the audience rose to their feet, erupting in applause. A standing ovation! I took a moment to soak up that feeling . . . it completely blew me away.

As an adult, my wife speaks at school assemblies all over Southern California. Together, we continue to speak about celebrating uniqueness. My wife gets the standing ovations now. My past has intertwined with her present.

# Chapter Four
## Double Dork

I<small>T WAS A</small> Saturday night in 1977, and even though I didn't know much about it, my friends had been talking about this movie called, *Star Wars*. Just *Star Wars*. The title wasn't *Episode IV Star Wars: A New Hope* like it is today. We stood in line, waiting with tons of other people as I tried to convince my friends to see something else. I didn't feel like waiting. But my friends insisted. I begrudgingly agreed, impatiently waiting until we finally made it into our seats.

The opening credits began and I was immediately sucked in. The long line, a distant memory, I couldn't take my eyes off the screen! I was headed into outer space, to a far-off galaxy, and I loved it! My bon bons were melting in my lap because I didn't want to miss a beat. Forget the popcorn and Milk Duds! I want to fight the Empire, meet Princess Leia, travel at light speed, and hang with Han Solo and Chewbacca.

*Star Wars* grabbed me because I felt like I was *there*—in the scene. The filmmaking was incredible. This was no hokie sci-fi movie. I felt as if I were actually riding in spaceships, battling bad guys, and talking to cool droids. The characters were fresh and new, the special effects were amazing—I didn't want the experience to end. The lights flickered on and I left the theater feeling pumped.

As I pulled out of the parking lot into the darkness, I flashed my high beams as if they were lasers and my car was an X-Wing fighter. Dork! My friends thought I was nuts, but I could tell they liked it.

I watched *Star Wars* again and again, bringing more friends to see what I had discovered. I was hooked and found myself, like so many others, anxiously awaiting the sequel, *The Empire Strikes Back*.

A few years later, when it was finally time, I promised my friends I wouldn't flash everyone in the parking lot with my high beams. I was, after all, a *little* more mature. As the movie ended, I stood up and shouted, "It's not over." But it was! I left the theatre wondering, *how could I have helped the rebels defeat Darth Vader*? Double Dork! If only I could have told my high school self, "Be patient. Someday you will."

# Chapter Five
# College

I STARTED PASADENA CITY College and knew I wanted to stick with theatre. I acted in many productions and was so dedicated that even after a surgery put me in a leg cast up to my thigh, I continued to climb the many stairs to my theatre classes. There was no elevator, so what could I do? Nothing could keep me from the theatre!

It wasn't long before I was invited by my professor to join his street mime troupe. A mime is an actor that creates a scene without the use of props or words. Everything is invisible and the actor uses his gestures and movement to make the audience believe that there is something there. The troupe was a group of approximately six actors that would go out into the streets performing mime techniques, both improv and scripted. The crowd would gather, and the street was our stage. The most physical thing about being a mime is trying to make it look like it's not physical. I had to make fluid motions from start to finish.

In my film classes I was making student films in front of the camera while also working behinds the scenes, on the crew. Since we students had to pay to produce our own films, I got my first taste of the cost of filmmaking. I also learned about the different aspects of making a film—availability, finance, location scouting, and most importantly, teamwork. One person not in sync on the crew could torpedo a project.

My point of view continued to be present in my films and my

classmates loved to mention it. The best films would be shown at the end of the semester in a film festival at the college. I made a film inspired by my experience climbing those stairs to theatre classes while in the cast called, *Stairway.* It came in 2nd place at the festival. I liked making films.

I started my professional career while attending college. I traveled with a musical comedy act, *The Original Harmonica Band.* That was an acting exercise for me—acting like I knew how to play the harmonica. I ended up being really good at it! And I did actually learn how to play harmonica. Most of the music was from the 1920's to the 1950's. The group even played the *Star Wars* theme, disco version. It was complete with the cantina music. The audience recognized it right away and would give us a big hand.

I liked the live theatre audience. I wish that Los Angeles were a theatre town like New York. When I was invited by a friend to try out for The Michael Dunn Theatre Group I jumped at the chance. It was housed in the Mark Taper Forum, which is part of the Music Center in Downtown Los Angeles. Many consider the Music Center to be the West Coast equivalent of Lincoln Center.

The Michael Dunn Theatre Group consisted of an all-Little People cast and I became one of them. The Music Center was given a grant to write, cast, and rehearse the project. We worked on it for several years with no pay, but a lot of training. We all had passion for the project and it fueled us. The project eventually folded and sadly, we never got to perform for an audience. But the experience was far greater than I could have ever imagined. I wouldn't trade it for anything.

As I focused more and more on my professional career, it became apparent to my college professors that my head was not on their courses. There was a wide world of entertainment at my feet. It was calling out to me and its pull was too strong to ignore.

# Chapter Six
## Getting in the Union

IBOOKED MY FIRST feature film at the same time I was able to buy myself an alcoholic beverage. It was the first film to cast the largest amount of Little People since The *Wizard of Oz*. *Under the Rainbow* with yours truly, and Carrie Fisher AKA Princess Leia.

I was a non-union extra, but after two weeks of training, I joined the stunt team. My gymnastic experience and imagination came in very handy. I swung from a chandelier, performed prêt falls (falls that are done on purpose, but look like an accident), and engaged in general mayhem. I had fun performing stunts—even though production did not call them stunts. Eager to get into the Screen Actors Guild (SAG), I kept asking if a particular stunt was SAG worthy and time after time, they would say, "No." This became an ongoing thing. Other people would have a line or a stunt and get into the union. I would not.

I kept performing the different gags and they kept enjoying my enthusiasm. On the last day of filming, I noticed a stand-in was to perform a stunt and get into the union. I was happy for her, but mad as heck at production. I lost it. I marched up to the producers and said very calmly, "It's great that you're giving the stand-in a stunt and she's getting in the union. I've performed more than a dozen stunts and you have refused to get me in. Why? Did I do something wrong? This just sucks." I turned around and left, sure that I would be fired.

I wasn't. One of the producers came up to me and apologized. "We actually thought you were in the union," he said, lying through his teeth. "We're over budget but I'll fill out this contract like we should have. You won't get paid for this, but it'll get you in the union." I begrudgingly agreed and focused on my win: I was now a SAG actor.

So, you might say that the Force was with me, because the next film I booked was *Blade Runner* with Harrison Ford, AKA Han Solo. Ridley Scott was the director and he wrote me my first on-screen line.

My first day on set was dark, wet, smoky, and in the middle of the night. We were in downtown Los Angeles. There were these rain machines, one hundred feet in the air that got me, along with at least one hundred extras, soaking wet. It wasn't glamorous, to say the least.

The environment really started getting to me. Cold, wet, tired— and breathing was tough because of the stage smoke. I soon felt like throwing in the towel. I took a short break and sat on the curb truly contemplating ditching my glamorous film actor life. An English gentleman came up to me and asked, "How are you doing?"

I briefly wondered; *does he really want to know?* But without giving it much thought I unloaded. All the pent-up anger and frustration inside poured out and the stranger simply listened.

Then he handed me a cup and said, "Have a sip."

Boy, howdy my sinuses opened up and it went down warming up my insides. He told me it was scotch. The good stuff. After recovering from the sting of that sip I asked, "What do you do?"

He introduced himself as the director. Ridley Scott.

*Wait. What?*

I tried to play it cool, even though I felt like crawling under the nearest rock. He kind of chuckled and we chatted for a bit. As I got over feeling mortified, he brought me a cup and we continued to share the rest of his scotch.

After that conversation I didn't complain anymore, even to myself. I also became more in tune with the people around me. Jordan Croneweth, the cinematographer, could barely walk. He never complained. He could run from set up to set up and the camera assistant would grab his chair and run after him. When Jordan got there, he would stop and fall backwards. The chair was always there in time. Who was I to complain about anything? Instead, I focused on the amazingness of what I was doing.

I guess Ridley and I bonded because he continued calling me back and wrote three parts for me: a mechanical toy bear, a street thug, and a smoking robotic clown. (My mime skills came into play for that one.)

Initially, Harrison Ford was quiet and to himself, but later warmed up to me. Ridley kept writing scenes for me. I felt very lucky even though the working conditions were difficult. I was in scenes with Rutger Howard, Edward James Olmos, and Darryl Hannah. They were all really nice. Ed was carrying around a personal film camera making his own home movies while being on set. At that time the film cameras were huge in size. It was four-hundred-feet reel to reel.

Remember how I said I was a SAG actor after I vented to production on *Under the Rainbow*? Even though I was officially in the union, I hadn't actually paid the five-hundred dollars required dues. Oops. I was taught the severity of this mistake one day when the Assistant Director informed me that I would get fired off *Blade Runner* unless I paid my dues to the union immediately. Apparently the sixty days I had to pay up were over and production would be fined if they continued to use me. So, at lunch I left the set and headed to the bank—still in costume—to get the cash. I put it in an envelope and handed it off to a Teamster who would deliver it to the guild. Now it was official! No fanfare, no trumpets, just a grumpy Teamster with another thing crossed off of his to do list. A Teamster's job is to drive anything and everything needed for production. They may haul equipment, livestock, people and yes, even envelopes full of cash.

By this time, my professors were kicking me out the door and my college days were over. But I was in the big leagues and my theatre professor was asking *me* for a job. Now all I had to do was wait for that next big call.

# Chapter Seven
## The Call

IT WAS TYPICAL sunny fall day in So Cal. I wanted to enjoy the day outside. As an actor, I am supposed to wait by the phone for it to ring. This leads to insanity. Sometimes I just stare at it, commanding it to ring. That usually doesn't work. It rings when I go out for an errand. Which, back then, living in a household of eight, was a major problem. I never knew if I would get the message. The telephone was a landline that the entire family shared and it lived in the most important and busiest room of the house—the kitchen. It was attached to the wall next to the door and had an extra long cord tethered to the receiver so one cold talk privately outside. There was a desk next to the phone that my mother called "a catch all" and boy did it catch all—paper, recipes, food wrappers, used Kleenex . . . gross!

That autumn day I stared at it, transfixed for who knows how long . . . but nothing happened. I walked into the other room . . . and it rang! I just happened to be the one that picked it up—lucky me!

On the other end of the telephone were casting agents Dave and Bill. I had worked with them on *Under the Rainbow*. They needed several agile Little People to audition for a movie, but they couldn't tell me the name of the movie or even the character I'd be auditioning for. This caught me off guard. How was I going to prepare for an audition without a character? The agents told me to wear something comfortable because it was very physical. I wrote the address down and hung up, my mind bursting with curiosity.

I tried, unsuccessfully, to push it out of my head. Many productions won't tell you the name of the picture, but they usually don't leave out the character. I would have to go into the audition cold. I guess I would just ad-lib. I kept an open mind. I had to. It could have been anything. The days leading up to that audition dragged on . . . I couldn't wait to find out more.

# Chapter Eight
## Moo

THE AUDITION WAS in Hollywood in the middle of the day (traffic hour, but then every hour is traffic hour). The address was a random old one-story office building without parking—not on a studio lot. I walked into the waiting room, all four-foot five-inches of me, and felt that familiar feeling: I'm instantly being sized up by the other actors in the room. It's a cattle call. That means everyone looks similar—whether they have acting skills or not, they all match the physical description. A quick look around and I notice that most of these cattle are people I know. It's a Little People cattle call. Dammit!

I saw the casting agents and shook their hands. Dave whispered that the role was right up my alley, and added, "Kev, you have a good chance."

I grabbed a pencil and signed in, trying not to get too excited. I asked, "What's the role?"

He acted like he didn't hear me and walked away. He turned back and yelled, "Don't forget to sign the non-disclosure form." A non-disclosure form means I cannot talk about the audition or the company will take legal action and sue me. I knew that meant it must be important!

I took a seat next to a group of people I knew from *The Hollywood Shorties*. I was so used to playing with these guys on the same team, but now we were playing against each other. It isn't easy vying for the same parts in Hollywood with people you like, especially when there aren't many parts written for Little People. I wanted to wish my friends well, but not too well. I wanted the job!

Just then the door slammed and out came another player from *The Shorties*. He was smiling and boasting about how well he felt about his audition. Of course, he did—he's from Texas. He is a little man from a big state where they wear cowboy boots and shiny belt buckles, so he put in a little more "filler and bull crap" in his big boots. We all asked him how it went and he just flashed a big 'ol smile. Classic psych out! You never know if the person before you really felt good or if they're just trying to mess you up. I learned quickly how fellow actors did this. Sometimes it was merely a cover to a bad audition. I had to shake it off! I wasn't the only one that wanted this mysterious job.

I started stretching and tried to loosen up to get my mind off things. I was ready to be hit with anything. One by one we all got our turn to audition and not a peep or clue was said by anyone. Nothing but smiles and nods all around. More people filled the waiting room as others left. I finally heard my name called. I had to stay calm and confident! I took a deep breath and the butterflies turned into excited caterpillars. I was ready!

Dave introduced me to Glenn Randall, Jr., a tall, tan, lean, and fit stuntman in his late forties. He really was the poster boy of stuntmen. He shook my hand with a firm grip and told me to call him J.R. He then pointed to the couch where Felix Silla, a friend of mine from *The Hollywood Shorties*, sat. Felix is a pituitary dwarf who is proportionate and is known in Hollywood to stunt double child actors. In his early forties, he had earned his place as a well-respected stunt actor and was there, helping out with the auditions.

J.R. asked if I knew Felix and I smiled and nodded. "We always have a good time working together. He's very funny and does his job well but gets grumpy when he gets tired and starts muttering under his breath. He has a strong Italian accent and the madder he gets the funnier he sounds." Everyone in the room started laughing.

We got to the meat of the audition. I proceeded to tell them about the stunts I did in *Under the Rainbow*. J.R. was interested in my work with the mini-trampoline, as a street mime, and in gymnastics. He asked me to show him some of my mime. I began with the classic "stuck in a glass box," "open a door," and "make a sandwich."

"Can you act like a monkey or a bear on two legs?" he asked.

I continued performing. Mime training taught me how to move and contort my body into different animals. He seemed entertained and wondered if I was afraid of heights. I ran around some more and then went full speed into the wall, fell into a back roll, went up into a handstand, and finished with a prêt fall on my stomach.

J.R. hit me with more questions. "Are you claustrophobic? Have you ever been in a full costume suit?"

I answered, "Not sure," and "Only on Halloween."

He told me the part was for an alien that was very physical. He also said the costume would cover from head to toe with a head, gloves, and feet. He didn't think the actors would be able to see much.

Remember how I did a lot of imaginary play? So now I challenged myself. I decided to run around the room again, but this time, with my eyes closed. J.R. was impressed. He threw different scenarios at me. "Act like a bear dodging bullets! Act like you're in a battle with other beings! And do that with your eyes closed and running!"

My imagination was being fed. It was like I was in my backyard again, having a blast. I ran, I rolled, I fell on the floor, jumped around, acted like a bear, an alien, and a monkey. Every time J.R. shouted out something new, I didn't miss a beat. Like improv partners who had worked together for years, we were completely in sync. It felt amazing.

When he finally yelled, "CUT!" I stopped in my tracks, exhilarated.

J.R. reminded me to sign that non-disclosure form. I was headed out the door when a heavy hand tapped my shoulder. It was J.R. "Are you really a mime and a gymnast?" he asked. I nodded. "I can't tell you if you got it, but think of this part as a cross between a bear and a monkey." He paused, flashed a small smile, and whispered, "See you soon." Then he turned away, disappearing back into the room.

I got in my 1972 Mercury Capri drenched in sweat. The audition had been so physical and my heart was beating fast. I cranked up the volume on the cassette player in the car. It was either Queen or Led Zeppelin, my two favorites at the time. My mind raced. I'd never had an audition like that before. Normally, I would be going over the whole thing, questioning every second of it. But this was different. I knew I had done well. I also knew I couldn't get too excited. But . . . I didn't notice J.R. walking any of my buddies out like he did with me. There were whispers that J.R. had worked with Steven Spielberg and George Lucas before. He only worked on big movies. Could this be the next *Star Wars*? One could only hope. I knew very little but one thing was clear: I had to be in this picture!

# Chapter Nine
## Non-Disclosure Form

FOR THE NEXT couple of days my full-time job was staring at the telephone. Every now and then I'd pick up the receiver, checking to make sure it still worked. I couldn't miss that call! My sister would get on the phone and be on too long—a minute was too long in my opinion. I would threaten to pounce on her like a cougar. The dirty looks were consistent. Why didn't she understand? Back then, there was no such thing as call waiting or texting. So, if someone were on the telephone when another call came in, the caller would simply get a busy signal. There was no way to leave a message. It was maddening. This couldn't happen to Spielberg, Lucas, or Obi Wan Kenobi. They wouldn't tolerate an obnoxious busy signal. I yelled at my sister, "GET OFF THE PHONE!"

I finally went outside to dribble the basketball. Leaving the telephone zone seemed to work yet again—before long, out came my sister. "You have a phone call," she said, kind of snotty.

I ran so fast I nearly tripped over my own two feet. Gripping the phone, I announced myself, trying my best to sound calm and collected. No big deal, right?

The voice on the other end said, "Hey Kevin, this is Dave . . . I'm just calling to tell you that you got it."

I GOT IT????

Whoa. Wait. Got what . . . the stunt actor or an extra performer? He told me that I beat out a lot of other people. I was one of only four who got the job. I could barely breathe! I still wasn't sure what the part was but in that moment what did it matter? I GOT IT!

Dave told me the working title was *Blue Harvest*, "But you know it as another name," he added.

I looked around my kitchen for spies and whispered, "*Star Wars?*"

He neither confirmed nor denied. It felt like Darth Vader was breathing down my neck. My hunch felt right. Dave said, "Get your passport . . . you're going to England and did you sign that non-disclosure form?" I DID!!!

I hung up the phone and looked over at my mother who was standing in the kitchen. I told her that I just booked a movie on what would be the biggest movie of the year. "That's nice, did you take out the trash?"

*Did I take out the trash?!* Clearly, she had no idea I was now a star. I didn't know what was in store for me, but I was ready for this journey to a galaxy far, far away.

Time passed slowly and I received different correspondence in the mail from *Blue Harvest*, but guess what? It also said *Lucasfilm!* I knew deep down this was the sequel, and dare I whisper, the long-awaited film in the *Star Wars* trilogy titled, *Revenge of the Jedi*. I couldn't tell anyone. I could only say that I was working on *Blue Harvest*. Remember, I signed that non-disclosure form!

I went on costume fittings in Los Angeles where they took my measurements, but there were no costumes or pictures. Everything was super secretive. I still didn't know what I would be wearing. Was it a bear or a monkey? I did learn the name of the character: an Ewok. The wardrobe people told me that I would be padded with foam and I'd be wearing fur. Hmmm . . . *Ewok.* J.R. had said it looked like a bear and lived in the trees like a monkey. Whatever it was, being an Ewok sounded like it was going to be hot, blind, and physical. I couldn't wait for more!

I applied for my very first passport and had it expedited.

Talk spread quickly through the Little People community. Everyone was anxious to find out who the four stunt actors were. Some people were speculating and others seemed to know but soon enough, the official word got out. The four stunt actors were Felix Silla, who was in the audition; Jimmy Briscoe, my buddy from *The Shorties*, an ex-clown from the circus and Billy Barty's stunt double; Bobby Porter who is a pituitary dwarf like Felix, but taller and younger; and yours truly, Kevin E. Thompson. That's me! Drop the mic! I was a kid at twenty-two-years old working in a man's world.

I was busting at the seams and desperately wanted to tell someone, but I couldn't even tell my family. This was no easy task. Coming from a big Catholic family, we gathered around the dinner table on Sundays. Everyone grabbed food and if you didn't get it when it passed by, you never saw it again. It was gone. Talk was loud and chaotic. We all understood one another even when we spoke simultaneously. There were no secrets because we all had the gift of gab, especially my father, the friendly pharmacist. Those family dinners were the toughest part of keeping my secret. But I couldn't say anything because I knew my family would spill the beans. They didn't sign that non-disclosure form . . . I did!

# Chapter Ten
## England, January 1982

JIMMY THE EX-CLOWN had a plan. His buddy was a limo driver and he would take us to the airport in style. We were feeling pretty good. Jimmy lived in a sketchy area at the base of the Hollywood Hills. But, because he knew his neighbors well, I parked on the street—he assured me that my car would be there when we got back from England. My bags and passport were packed.

We waited and waited and waited. Our limo driver never showed. We grabbed our things, jumped in my car, and high tailed it to the airport. The freeway was jammed so we got off and took side streets. Jimmy was the co-pilot-slash-navigator and I was the stunt driver. Green lights were our friend and I was trying to catch them all. I would turn left or right depending on the traffic in front of me. I didn't care what was behind me until I ran into a construction zone and had to put the car in reverse. I slammed on the brakes. Jimmy almost flew through the windshield. His cigarette was now lodged in his nose. Good thing it wasn't lit. That would teach him to wear his seatbelt.

Weaving in and out of traffic I tried to keep moving toward the airport. The flight was scheduled to leave in less than one hour. We ended up in a long-term parking lot; we flagged a shuttle and checked into the international terminal. I was so afraid. Was I really going to miss this chance of a lifetime because I was late?

We made it through security and up to the gate where we found Felix, Bobby, and J.R. sitting, relaxed and ready to go. They gave the look and said things like, "Glad you could make it," and "We weren't sure if you were going to get on this flight." We didn't know either, but we didn't let them know that. Jimmy and I were highfaluting actors now and we had been in our own circus that day.

J.R. congratulated each one of us since we hadn't seen him since our audition. Once we got on the airplane, he revealed more. "This is going to be a lot of work with more work in April."

Hold the bus . . . were we staying in England through April? I had only packed one week's worth of underwear! I wished I had a talent agent to let me know these things . . . I had booked the gig freelance. Communication had been directly with Dave and Bill. The highfaluting actor playing a bear-like monkey was sitting in economy class with only a week's worth of underwear headed to England for who knows how long!

J.R. explained that we were going to England for fittings and to get to know the costumes. The costumes were made specifically for stunts so each one had to be customized for us. The four of us would not be filmed on set in London. The really hard work would be in April when filming began in Northern California amongst the Redwood Forest. I made a mental note: *keep April open*. Well, I was happy to do that! Being twenty-two years old on a flight going far, far away, I had no worries. I was on an adventure with friends and I couldn't wait for the mysteries of the film to be revealed. I was feeling the fish-n-chips with a pint. England, here I come!

Felix and Bobby had worked with J.R. before on the films, *ET* and *Poltergeist*. J.R. had a reputation of wanting a ton of mega action. They told me I would be very busy. We swapped fish stories and told jokes with a little shut-eye in between. It was tough to sleep on a plane with so much excitement.

We landed in London around five o'clock in the evening. J.R. had a long stride walking through the airport, and the four of us little guys had to run to keep up with him. I am sure we caught a lot of stares with one tall stuntman and the four of us eagerly trotting behind him.

The weather was the typical London fog that so many people talk about. It was cold and wet. We met our driver and went to our hotel, which was quite nice. Five stars! Crystal chandeliers! I had definitely hit the big time. It even had a full bar in the lobby, which I thought was pretty amazing, even though it wasn't up to Jimmy's standards. "No Coors?! You've gotta be kidding me."

All I could really think about was getting to the set the following day. Elstree Studios had the largest stage in the world and that is where I wanted to go. I wanted to meet Mr. George Lucas. Tomorrow was a big day. How would I ever get to sleep?

# Chapter Eleven
## Elstree Studios

ELSTREE STUDIOS IS twenty miles east of London in a town called Boreham Wood. The studio was made to get away from the infamous smog of the big city of London. It was built in the 1920s and put out many movies, just like the Hollywood Studios.

George Lucas had filmed both *Star Wars* and *The Empire Strikes Back* at Elstree Studios. Stepping out of the car, I instantly felt the history of the place. It was hallowed ground and it vibrated with an indescribable energy.

As we approached the stage door J.R. sarcastically said, "These little English blokes are in for a surprise. You guys are going to be a real hit." He let out a hardy laugh. Stuntwomen and men are some of the biggest practical jokers in the world. I had a feeling we were about to be served to the lions.

The door opened and my eyes adjusted to the set. All I could see were redwood trees. Beyond the man-made trees was a photo backdrop, making the forest appear endless. Up above was the enormous Ewok village. Huts were built in the branches of each tree with swinging rope bridges connecting them. Nothing but thirty-foot high platforms held up the set and there was a freight elevator and stairs leading up to the platforms.

The crew was busy and production was in full swing. Four actors, the same size as us, were walking and talking to each other when we caught their eye. They gave us a look that said they were not expecting us and… they didn't look too thrilled to see us.

J.R. laughed and said, "I told you that you guys were going to be a hit." Apparently, the little English blokes had been fighting to do the stunt work themselves. Our sudden appearance sent the message: they had lost the fight.

We took the elevator up and J.R. gave us a quick tour then led us to an area where the English actors were resting. All the Ewok village scenes were shot in England with local actors. The Ewok battle scenes would later be filmed in Northern California with American actors. This was the first time I saw a full Ewok costume with an actor inside. It was much fatter than I had imagined. We were the only Little People *not* dressed in the Ewok costumes and we stood out, looking like American tourists.

J.R. introduced us to Richard Marquand (the director) and George Lucas (the creator). They shook our hands, asked how our flight was, and welcomed us to Endor, the planet the Ewoks lived on. I replied with the weather. I couldn't believe it . . . I was introduced to Richard Marquand and George Lucas and I talked about the weather!

We chatted with other members of the crew, and when the scene finished, the Ewok actors took off their costume heads revealing red and sweaty human faces. Without a wave, smile, or hello, the little English blokes walked toward the holding area to rest.

One little actor asked if we were new recruits or if we were just visiting. I spoke up, maybe a little too excited and said, "We're the American stuntmen who are going to do your stunts." Record scratch. Crickets. Everyone seemed to freeze in place. We were pelted with stares from all the local Ewoks.

I guess that wasn't the right thing to say?

Jimmy whispered, "Way to go, Bub."

Bobby stepped in to my rescue and added, "It was going to happen anyway, Kevin just sped things up."

We took the moment to properly introduce ourselves. J.R.

thoroughly enjoyed the show of American Ewok actors verses English Ewok actors. We didn't need to hear him laughing to know he was entertained. We moved on to wardrobe.

The wardrobe people were very excited to see us and were a much more welcoming group. They showed us sketches and discussed our scenes. It looked like we would be running and jumping out of trees. We began asking questions. "What do the Ewok feet look like? Will we be able to run in them? How about the hands? Will we be able to grip and hold ourselves up in the trees? Will we be able to see with the heads on?" They assured us that we were all on the same team and that we would work together ironing out all the glitches with the costumes.

We started with the feet. They were soft, spongy slippers with three big toes in the front. We tried them on and the group decided it would be best for us to have athletic shoes that gave us more stability for running and jumping. The wardrobe people would make fur coverings and feet to go over the shoes.

Our Ewok hands were spongy too and we all agreed it was too hard to grip things. They were designed with three fingers, like a fat trident. I could put two of my fingers in one of the costume fingers of the Ewok. We needed something more pliable with a grip.

While listening to the creative wardrobe department and seeing all their sketches of the costumes, colors, and props, I started daydreaming about Ewoks battling. I was in my backyard again, playing on the swing set, fighting off the bad guys . . . then suddenly, *Ouch.*

Jimmy hit me in the head, bringing me back to earth and interrupting my very exciting backyard battle. He had been given a shopping list from the wardrobe department. I didn't know if it was just to appease us after all our questions, or if these items would actually help us feel more confident in doing our stunts. We went out on a mission for athletic shoes and gloves.

The typical man way of shopping is to get in and out as quickly as possible. We all found our shoes and gloves easily. We brought them back to wardrobe and were finished for the day.

Our driver took us back to the hotel and we decided to take in the sights of London. We walked to Big Ben, the Parliament Building, and Buckingham Palace. We looked around for Piccadilly Circus and we didn't know we were already walking around in it. We were American tourists after all, and as much as I hate to admit it, we were looking for a real circus. You would think Jimmy, a professional clown, would have had a clue about what Piccadilly Circus was. Egad!

Lunch was a mistake because we ordered American hamburgers. It wasn't like an American hamburger. It didn't taste like beef. I think it was pressed pigeon. I should have ordered the fish and chips. First London lesson learned. I was already becoming worldy!

# Chapter Twelve
## Inquisitive English Friend

APART FROM THE whole catching the local Ewoks off guard with our arrival thing, our first day seemed pretty successful. As we began our second day at Elstree Studios an inquisitive young boy, who was an Ewok with the most proper English accent, said, "Hello, I wanted to meet you. They say you are the stuntmen." We were finally greeted with a friendly local Ewok face!

We nodded and the twelve-year-old proper little English man proceeded to tell us that he wanted to be a stuntman! He had a list of questions for all of us – he wanted to know our credits, stunt skills, sizes, and what we ate for breakfast. His name was Warwick Davis. The kid was a bundle of excitement and couldn't seem to hold anything back. He was exactly what we needed.

A crowd started gathering and the other local Ewoks listened in on our conversation. Through Warwick's questioning, they learned we had experience and had earned the job. We weren't some random American actors that just happened to fit in the costume. We were all trained in our profession. Soon Warwick's little interview turned into a sort of open forum, with everyone tossing out questions. We were having a great time, sharing stories and laughter. We would have continued, but the production assistant broke it up. There was work to be done. We headed over to the make-up department.

We entered with Mr. Stuart Freeborn. He had been a make-up artist since 1936 and was the man that designed all the *Star Wars* aliens. He looked like Yoda, only a little taller. He was a soft-spoken guy and said, "Hello, so you are the stuntmen who are to make the Ewoks come alive and save the rebels."

Wow!

Jimmy, Bobby, Felix and I looked at each other silently asking, "Did he just give us a short rundown of the whole picture?"

Stuart gave us a pre-made Ewok head to try on. It was made of latex/rubber and had fur all around it. It covered our entire heads from front to back with a Velcro strip to close in the back. The Ewok costumes had hoods that covered the seam and the neck opening in the back. The mouth had no fur and was slightly ajar with fake teeth in the front. The nose looked like a dog's nose and the eyes were plastic brownish spheres, made to look like an animal's eyeballs. The eyeballs ended up being my worst enemy. But more on that later.

The stunts would be dangerous if the heads didn't fit properly, so Stuart decided to make custom head casts for each of us. I was excited and a little nervous – I had never had one made before. Stuart's son, who was also a trained make-up artist, led the charge and proceeded to work on mine.

First, they covered my hair with a latex bald cap. Our faces were clean-shaven so that no plaster would stick to our facial hair. My face was slathered with Vaseline and then strips of plaster bandages were applied with water. (These are the same types of strips doctors use to cast a broken arm or leg.) They started at the top of my head then moved to the back, leaving my face for last. Straws were placed in my nose and mouth so that I could breathe while they plastered as close as possible to the openings. The plaster strips started to get warm and heavy as they set. The room turned dark.

I'm glad I am not claustrophobic. It was a strange experience. Stuart's son talked to me every step of the way with reassurance. I couldn't do anything to protect myself and I was nervous someone walking by would bump the straws further up my nose and mouth! All

I could hear were muffled conversations because my ears were covered, too. I just sat there trying to convince myself that I was at a spa having a facial. (Even though I haven't been to a spa—yet!) I sat there for approximately twenty minutes while it hardened.

Once it was completely dry, I was told to move my eyebrows and slowly wiggle my face to loosen the plaster. They divided the front and back by cutting up the sides of the cast by my temples and up to the top of my head. I took in the sight of it. There it was - the front and back of my head, in two pieces. It was eerie to see a replica of myself. Did I really look like that?

These English guys were funny men. They joked saying, "We have to do it again." Ugh! And then they smiled to let me know that they were kidding. It really wasn't as bad as I thought it would be, but I was happy to be done.

Being the youngest of the stuntmen, I didn't have patience to wait for the others to finish up with their head casts so I strolled… okay maybe I ran, back to the set. I saw a face that I had seen in the movie *Time Bandits*… it was Kenny Baker. Then I saw Jack Purvis and Mike Edmonds too. I struck up a conversation and they gave me some tips on how to stay cool. Not like cool, wearing dark shades driving a Ferrari, like cool as in not hot. "It would be good to keep up your water intake. The costume is very cumbersome." They looked me in the eye and told me that it was a job and they were thankful to have it. It was time for their scene, so they headed off to get suited up in their Ewok costumes.

I was excited to see them in action. I watched their movements and it gave me ideas. The facial movements were very restricted by the way the heads were made, so everything had to be expressed through body movements. As a trained mime, I start imitating these movements. I was off to the side, totally engrossed in mimicking their movements.

Jimmy and Bobby startled me after the director yelled, "Cut." I had no idea they were standing behind me, ready to pounce. They were eager to see what was going on too!

On every set there is a glorious area called craft service. It's where all meals are served and snacks and coffee are always at the ready. The higher the budget of the movie, the better the snacks. It might consist of cheese and crackers or soup and lobster. This one wasn't too shabby. The three of us headed over to get a snack and there was Carrie Fisher. She was wearing a brown suede dress and her hair was long with a small braid. It was her Endor dress. She smiled and said, "Hey, I know you guys," and gave us all big hugs. She remembered us from *Under the Rainbow*.

Carrie was friendly and welcoming. We watched as she went back to work and did her scene with Mark Hamill. It was the famous scene when they are on the bridge on Endor and she discovers they're brother and sister. OMG!! Another major plot point revealed!

Production told us we were done for the day and sent us back to the hotel. I wondered if we, the American stuntmen, were causing a stir, because they kept sending us back to the hotel. I tried not to take it personally and we decided to head out to enjoy some more sightseeing while we had the time.

# Chapter Thirteen
## Friends

ON DAY THREE, our friend Warwick greeted us with that same excitement and joy. Our little friend was so proper he remembered all our names. The other Ewok actors greeted us as well. We had to be doing something right. It was starting to feel like home. We were having such a great time that production broke it up. They had a scene to shoot and we had to go to wardrobe.

When we arrived at wardrobe, they had made new padding for us that wasn't as thick as the two-inch foam on the other Ewok costumes. It was a one-piece quilted jumpsuit. We all tried them on. It was much easier to move around in and not as hot as the foam. I jumped up and down, rolled on the floor, and ran around testing it out. It was decided that the quilted jumpsuits would be outfitted for the stuntmen costumes.

I chatted with my wardrobe gal and asked her why the change of heart with the other local Ewoks. They seemed much friendlier towards us. She said they had realized we were real stuntmen. At first, they thought we were Americans there just to take their jobs. She also said that Warwick had been talking about us to anyone who would listen and was saying all kinds of nice things.

I guessed we would have to thank him. It's true what they say, "out of the mouth of babes." The young are innocent and speak the truth.

We left wardrobe pretty confident that we had accomplished everything they needed from us. It was our last day on set in London and we were set to leave the next morning. The next time we would try on the Ewok costumes we'd be back in California.

It was time for lunch so we went to the commissary. A commissary on the studio lot is much like a cafeteria. It is for employees so they don't have to leave the premises to find an eating establishment. As we entered, we were surprised to find a bar that served alcohol, because back in the states our commissaries did not serve alcohol. Everyone was having a drink with their lunch. The local Ewoks called us over and boy, were they in a chipper mood. Maybe it was the alcohol, but we took them up on their invite and sat with them. They asked us about Hollywood, our families, and for stories about the states. Warwick walked up and I personally thanked him for being the bold one who broke the ice for us. He gave me this look and I knew that this proper little young man was just being himself. I remember hoping he would stay that way forever and I knew we would meet again.

It was time to say our goodbyes just when it was going so well. The saying goes "leave them wanting more." We hoped we would see them when filming began in California, but no one knew who would be invited to continue. It was time to pack our bags and get a good night's sleep so we'd be ready to catch our plane early the next morning.

On the flight home, I sat with Jimmy in the smoking section. Me, being a non-smoker, couldn't take it for very long. England was not like California where there were smoking and non-smoking sections. People smoked everywhere and they were the majority, so I had had my fill. I told Jimmy I had to move, got up, and found a seat next to Bobby in the non-smoking section.

Bobby shared a secret that he had bottled up the whole week and told me we weren't going to be needed until late April or even May. He also said that we might not even be called at all because we weren't on a contract yet—production might not even use us. I hadn't given much thought to that idea being that I was only twenty-two years old and still living at my parent's house, but Bobby had a family of his own. He confessed he had a chance to be the stunt coordinator and work twice as long on another feature film. He would make twice the money and it would be a promotion for him. It would be silly not to do it, but of course anyone who is in show business knows it's hard to let one job go for another—especially since it was rare to grab a feature like this one. He gave me a wink and said, "It'll benefit you because you'll get all my stunts." I didn't know what to say. I was stunned. Bobby didn't tell anyone else and I had to keep it to myself. It was a long fourteen hours home on the plane. I couldn't wait for April.

We finally landed in Los Angeles and got off the plane. We said good-bye to Bobby and Felix and then Jimmy and I headed out together. All we wanted to do was get home. Jimmy told me to get my keys out of my bag . . . SNAG. I couldn't find my keys! I tried to stay calm and I emptied my bag out all over the baggage claim floor.

No keys!

This fresh-faced stuntman left his keys in London. I called my dad to tell him about his stranded world traveler. Anyone who knows Jimmy will know that he was now headed to the bar *and* he would not let me forget this incident for a long time, if ever. While Jimmy was at the bar, I was out on the curb waiting for my dad to bring my spare keys. He got there with a halfhearted, "Welcome home, you idiot." I love my dad!

I found Jimmy and we got in the car. I dropped him off at his apartment and we said our goodbyes. I headed home unable to stop thinking about what Bobby had said to me on the plane. I started to worry that maybe I wouldn't be in the film because I didn't have a contract for April yet. All the fittings and head casts and gloves and quilted one-piece jumpsuits may all have been for nothing. I thought the Force was with me. Ugh! I wanted this job! I needed to be in the *Star Wars* family! I knew Harrison Ford from *Blade Runner*. I knew Carrie Fisher from *Under the Rainbow*. Everything was lined up, even the stars and planets. It was kismet! I had to stay hopeful!

# Chapter Fourteen
# Blue Harvest

As the weeks dragged on, there was talk amongst the Little People about Lucasfilm looking for extras for a film called *Blue Harvest*. I knew what that meant and the ad said they were looking for agile Little People. All of a sudden, I was everyone's friend because they knew I had been in London for this same feature. They asked me what it was about, what kind of costume I had worn, and if it was strenuous. I didn't know what to tell them, and if I could even tell them anything because of that non-disclosure form. That form gave me nightmares. *And* it really cramped my style. I am a talker and I couldn't talk. Not even after Bobby told me about his secret. I had become a secret keeper and it did not suit me!

Casting agents Dave and Bill had remained in contact with most of the Little People from *Under the Rainbow*. Most Little People were not in the entertainment business and held regular jobs. Since the filming would be five to six weeks in Northern California, they would have to take a leave of absence.

The casting for additional Ewoks proved to be difficult because many people who were originally cast ended up backing out. There was a constant rotation of people committing and then not committing. Jimmy was cast in a foreign film in Italy, so he backed out too. I could only imagine what was going on in the casting department. Little People don't grow on trees, you know.

As the days passed, I continued to remain hopeful without getting *too* confident. Would I be continuing on? Nobody told me I wouldn't be, but nobody told me I would either. Each bit of correspondence I received brought me closer and closer but part of me felt I couldn't believe it until I was back on set.

Four months after returning from London, I happily boarded a plane for Northern California to begin filming!

It must have been a sight to see approximately thirty-five Little People on the same plane from Los Angeles. Everyone was excited. Dave and Bill were on the airplane doing a head count. Even though Felix and I were the only ones from the "Original American Stuntman Group," I knew all the extra Ewoks from *Under the Rainbow* and *The Shorties*. There were local Little People actors in the mix along with a couple of ex-clowns as well as a bunch of carefree nine-to-five workers who took a leave from their regular jobs to get out of the office and make a little money.

But three of the guys hired were good friends of mine. They would ultimately make up my closest group throughout my adventure: Tony Cox, Chris Romano, and Michael Gilden. We had played on *The Shorties* together and already functioned as a team. I had known Michael since I was a kid. He was a few years younger than me and lived in my neighborhood. Tony was a devout Christian from Alabama who was skilled in martial arts and Chris was a gym rat from Michigan.

We changed planes in San Francisco to a little puddle jumper that took us further north to Eureka, California. We landed in Eureka and boarded a bus to the production office in Crescent City, California. There, we filled out paper work and received our per diems. A per diem is a daily cash allowance for food and sundries when you are shooting out of town. We were in the middle of nowhere and we weren't even at our destination yet. Next stop: Brookings, Oregon.

We jumped back on the bus and went to our hotel. Brookings was a small lumber town on the coast of Oregon. Though we would be shooting in California, we were staying just across the state line in Oregon. The production was so large that we took up all the surrounding area hotels. Other cast and crewmembers were splintered in Crescent City and Smith River, but it was just us Little People in Brookings. We had the entire hotel, called *The Thunderbird*, to ourselves. It really was more of a motel because there were no interior hallways. The doorways led to the outside with a large parking lot just beyond our doors.

*The Thunderbird* was the best of the bunch because we had access to everything we could need. There was a diner, a restaurant with a bar and dance floor (and live entertainment!), a convenience store, and a laundromat all within walking distance. The rooms were simple—my corner room had just a bed, table, and chair. For me, the sink was up to my chest and I could only see myself from the neck up in the mirror without a stool. (My typical point of view into a mirror over a standard height sink.) I thought about my shorter friends and how they would have to accommodate. There wasn't a coffeemaker, microwave, or refrigerator with a wet bar—this was definitely not London—but the view outside my window was beautiful . . . a meadow with large evergreen trees.

I unpacked my clothes into the brown circa 1970's dresser and put my sundry items in the bathroom. Since I would be staying for a couple of weeks, I tried to make it cozy. A bunch of us went to the nearby diner, which was the definition of small-town charm. The staff was very friendly, it was clean, and the food was good and inexpensive. Even though I was a high fallutin stuntman, I had to watch my spending. In my twenty-two-year-old mind, I was making big money. This was not chore money from my mom!

After dinner, we all headed back to our rooms, tired from travel. Tomorrow was our first day of rehearsal and we didn't know what to expect. All we *did* know was that production was sending someone to pick us up in the morning. Then it would be time to work!

# Chapter Fifteen
## Primitive Aliens

WE WAITED OUTSIDE *The Thunderbird* for our ride. I expected a town car, but what pulled up was something very different—an old yellow school bus. It was clean, but worn. This school bus was going to be our friend. We boarded it to find our out-of-town English friends. Their introduction to the American Little People was a lot easier than our surprise introduction back in London.

Our friend Warwick was on the bus with another Little Person his age. Warwick was the most intriguing friend. He warmed up the crowd by explaining the history of the Ewoks. I wish I had been in his first meeting with George Lucas. That would have been fun because Warwick was full of questions, excitement, and ideas that probably intrigued George. Warwick told us the Ewoks were like primitive men, but animal-like. They used rudimentary tools and had a common language amongst themselves. The Ewoks were named after the Native American tribe, the Miwok. They lived in the redwood forest in close proximity to our location. Warwick and his friend were to play younger Ewoks, but Warwick was the alpha male on the bus with all his stories. The English actors were just smiling and nodding at everything Warwick said because they had worked with him in the village scenes back in London. Needless to say, the half hour bus ride to rehearsal went by fast.

The rehearsal room was a large dance hall in a local roadhouse tavern. Rehearsals were used as conditioning to get us all in shape because the work would be strenuous. There, we met Wendy, our choreographer. Wendy was a fit, energetic woman and she made the work fun. We stretched and ran around in our workout clothes and later, she taught us Ewok movements.

The English Ewoks filled us in on the costumes and what kind of movements we would be able to do and not do. They explained that the fat suits with the two-inch padding moved with the body more than just our arms and legs. We had to use our entire bodies to move. Their biggest tip was that the costumes were always HOT. We practiced every day and it quickly became apparent who was serious and more in shape. Some were better actors with our pretend play and others were just there for the experience.

The costumes for the American Ewoks got mixed up in transport from London. This was an additional headache the wardrobe department did not expect. Everyone now needed to be fitted again. One by one we had our costume fittings and each person would come back with stories about what their costume looked like. Each Ewok had their own signature look, only for the trained eye though, as most of the costumes were brown. The fur was similar to a cats. Some had stripes or splotches, while others were solid shades. I couldn't wait for my turn. I wanted to see what my fur looked like!

My Ewok costume was brown with a white slash across the face and right eye. I was the only one with this signature slash. I wondered if my mother would be the only one who could tell who I was.

I tried on my Ewok head and it fit perfectly. The only constriction was the teeth and eyes. I would have to work with that. But I was glad to have had my head cast done back in London, because the extras didn't have that. Later, when it was time for stunts, I realized what a luxury having that custom head was.

I tried on the rest of my costume. I had to first put on foam leg pieces that looked like pork chops. They slid up my entire leg, from my hip down to my ankle. It was one foam piece for each leg that didn't have much give when it came to bending at the knee. My upper body was one piece of foam that had arms attached to the torso. It was put on over my head like a stiff, long sleeved t-shirt. This was what made the Ewoks so rotund.

Next step was the one-piece fur jumpsuit that covered all the foam. The fur suit had a zipper and snaps. The fur fit snuggly over the foam, which made it move with our bodies. We all had wardrobe assistants to help us suit up. It was not easy, to say the least. It was a real chore to put the costume on. I always put on my suit legs first and wiggled the fur up around my bottom then top. My shoulders and arms were last with the assistant closing up the seams with the zipper and snaps. They then brushed the fur over the zipper so it became invisible. I could not get out of the costume by myself. I was trapped as an Ewok!

The assistants put on the latex gloves and feet—they were a great fit. I was curious about my stunt feet that covered my tennis shoes we had bought in London. I tried them on and the tennis shoes were now very tight once the fur was put over the shoes. The stunt gloves were snug, too. I felt a little nervous. There was no place or time to get a bigger size shoe or gloves in this forest town. My shoe size was very hard to find.

Last step, was the head. Once that was on, I was fully suited up. Remember what I had said about the eyes becoming enemy number one? They started fogging up immediately with my body heat even before I started to move! The wardrobe assistants asked me how I felt and if I could move around. I knew had to make it work.

I started to walk around, slowly moving my legs up and down. I felt like I was in a doctor's office for a physical evaluation. I moved my arms, but with some restriction. I then fell down on the floor to see if I would be able to get up. I startled the wardrobe assistants at first, but I knew it could be detrimental if I couldn't get up by myself. Thankfully, I could, with a lot of muscle, but it gave me some peace of mind.

With the head on, my ears were covered. The Ewok ears were actually placed on top of the head, way above my actual ears, so sounds were muffled by fur. I could understand what people were saying, but I really had to listen. With the eyes being fogged up, all I could see were images or shadows. I really had to concentrate.

I had a second Ewok head that I would use strictly while performing stunts. Everything was much softer and more pliable. The teeth in the face were made of soft rubber rather than hard resin. This was a safety precaution just in case I did a face plant. That way, the resin teeth wouldn't impale me. The eyes were removable in the stunt heads, but our actual eyes were seen under the heads when they removed them so they had to keep the costume eyes in.

The undressing part of the costume was a little faster than the dressing. We started in reverse order. The head came off and then the rest. I quickly learned what the others had said about the costumes being hot. I was already drenched in sweat from head to toe. And this was only my fitting - we hadn't even started working yet! I thought, *Wow what was it going to be like when we are in the forest running around with explosives?*

The wardrobe assistants wanted me to try on the stunt suit. They give me a towel to dry off, and proceeded with the quilted one-piece jumpsuit to replace the typical Ewok foam or fat suit. The quilted one-piece was much easier to put on. I could almost put it on myself. The same fur was put back on over the quilted suit, but it wasn't as snug against it. I noticed that the wardrobe designer was not happy with the look. It did look different than the foam fat suit, but I could move so much easier. With the quilted suit, the body heat wasn't as intense so my eyes did not fog up as quickly. I really wanted to use this suit more than the foam.

The whole outfit was removed and I felt like I had just come out of the sauna. I felt bad for the poor assistants who had to take the Ewok costumes off us. Yuck. I noticed red splotches on my feet from the tennis shoes being so tight. The wardrobe department said they would try to stretch the shoes and put in a little material padding. The padding would only make it tighter, but hopefully it wouldn't rub on my skin. Talcum powder became everyone's friend.

Now that everyone had tried on their full Ewok costumes in their final fittings, the talk in the rehearsal hall became a reality of things to come. Some Little People only had about an eight-inch inseam and once the foam padding and fur were on them it decreased their inseam by at least two inches. A raccoon has an inseam that size. Only a raccoon can see in the dark and has a full set of fingers. We Ewoks weren't so lucky.

# Chapter Sixteen
# Yellow School Bus

OUR YELLOW SCHOOL bus was waiting, ready to take us back to our home away from home. It reminded me of a typical elementary school bus. Our driver was a union Teamster who had several years under his belt. He had grey wispy hair and greeted all of us with a big smile. He got to know all of our names. I wish I could remember his. I'll call him Tommy.

There were no seat belts and this gave us the opportunity to move around while the bus was in motion. Anytime he would slam on the brakes, we'd go flying toward the front. No one got hurt, but our egos wilted. The flyer would then get teased all the way to our destination. It became part of our daily routine. Cliques starting forming and different groups sat together in the back of the bus like cool kids. The front of the bus was for the talkative ones that loved chatting with Tommy. And the middle of the bus was a free for all. The rides were sometimes really loud and sometimes very quiet.

On the first ride back to the motel after our final fittings, everyone was full of emotion. Whether they were excited or scared, they had a lot to say—mostly about the costumes. Two people realized that the job and costumes were not for them, so they ended up leaving the next day.

When we arrived back to the motel Marty, the owner, was putting up a backboard and basketball hoop. The parking lot would soon be a basketball court! We were so excited. Marty was like Santa caught in the act. He had wanted to surprise us with it up and have it ready, but we came back early. He seemed a little disappointed, but not us! Thrilled, we threw our bags to the side and looked for the ball.

Tony shot first and . . . *swish*! Point. He declared himself king of the court! Nobody argued and Tony, Chris, Michael, and I stayed and played two-on-two while the others went back to their rooms to rest . . . and contemplate their costume and whether or not they could handle it. Marty stayed and watched us, wearing a huge grin. We gave him big thanks and played until nightfall. It was a really nice gesture—the perfect thing for us to let off steam during our downtime. We planned on putting it to good use.

Our first week consisted of traveling on our yellow school bus to rehearsals, conditioning our bodies, and really getting to know each other. Evenings became a routine with groups meeting for poker, basketball, conversation, and other common interests. Some even held hands. I guess love was in the air. It was like camp away from home. It was really neat to watch.

# Chapter Seventeen
## Stunt Training

J.R. TOLD FELIX and I that Bob Yerkes would be training us on a Russian swing, ropes, and mini trampolines. Bob was a known stuntman from the circus, and he trained people in his own backyard on trapeze and swings. A Russian swing is a swinging platform that two or more people stand on. It rotates three hundred-sixty degrees around the top of an A-frame cross bar attached with steel bars rather than rope. The momentum is the same as a child's swing, it is gained by pumping your own body weight.

J.R. also told us that he needed to recast Bobby and Jimmy for stunts because they had left. He also needed additional agile people. We gave him some names and he watched them in rehearsals. Then he chose eight people to join Felix and me to train with Bob Yerkes. I was thrilled when three of them were my buddies, Tony, Chris, and Michael. Later, he would choose four to join the stunt team. I hoped my friends would make the cut.

It was fun being introduced to circus work. The Russian swing was amazing. Bob would be on it with two little guys in the front. He did all the pumping because he knew exactly what speed and height would work best. Originally, we jumped off and flipped a somersault onto an airbag, much like diving into a swimming pool. He realized that it was not going to be a stunt we could do with the costumes, but it got us familiar with flying and flipping in the air. We learned to bring our legs in front of us at the same time we jumped off the swing, so that it would look like we were jumping out of the tree and onto stormtroopers.

After the training sessions, J.R. chose four people to come aboard the stunt team. Yes! Chris, Michael, and Tony were three of them! Tony was also named as the stunt double for Warwick Davis. Because Warwick was a child, he couldn't do anything dangerous and had limited hours for work because he had to go to school. Our stunt team was now complete.

During our time with Bob Yerkes we met the average size stuntmen who would be playing the rebels and stormtroopers. Sometimes, depending on the day, the same stuntman would play both characters. When the fight scenes were filmed there were times when the stuntmen would actually forget what team or character they were portraying and battle it out with their own teammate. They had just finished their stunts on Jabba's barge in Yuma, Arizona a week previously. Many of the guys got hurt there, so those that were working with us were the lucky ones that made it through.

While rehearsing with the stuntmen, we were only in our gym clothes. We moved around, miraculously agile and with impeccable timing. I knew things would be very different once we put on our rotund and restricting Ewok costumes.

Later that day, we climbed into a van to go and rehearse outdoors. This would be my introduction to the Forest Moon of Endor. We rode toward the small town of Smith River and onto a dirt road. It wound through the tall trees and down into a valley for miles. I couldn't tell you where we were, but it was magical.

There was a man that looked like Shaggy from Scooby Doo and he even had a van like the Mystery Machine. He was the guard that knew the comings and goings on this private road. He carried a walkie-talkie for communication. There was a barbed wire fence that was rolled to the side. You would never know that a multi-million-dollar production was on site. The only hint was the thirty-five Little People who suddenly appeared in town, wining and dining at all the local establishments. That was a lot of dwarfs in one place. The circus didn't even have that many dwarfs under the big tent (dwarfs and circuses are an urban legend, for your information).

We stepped out of the van. The crisp air and the smell of dirt and wood were refreshing after our two weeks in the rehearsal halls. The fine details of Endor were not added yet, but we were amongst godly trees that stretched above the clouds, enormous boulders, and deep green ferns that looked like they were on steroids. They were huge. Everything was huge.

We practiced running on fallen tree logs and swinging on ropes that looked like vines. The best part was landing into twelve-inch crash pads! I felt great. With more Little People contracted for stunts, the testosterone was kicking in and the competition was fierce. We were having a blast trying to outdo one another.

As the days took us closer to shoot our scenes, the excitement grew and grew. The main cast had arrived from Yuma and they were filming the speeder bike scenes throughout the forest. We didn't know what a speeder bike was, but it sounded very cool. We overheard production conversations about the special effects that would make them come alive. The blue screen work would be done at ILM (Industrial Light and Magic) Studio in San Rafael, California. A blue screen is used to layer two-images of film on top of each other to create a background without actually being there. One screen would be filmed on stage with an actor on a speeder bike pretending to ride without the bike actually moving and the second-screen layer would be the exterior shot of riding through the forest at high speed.

Garrett Brown, the cameraman, used his invention, a steadicam. A steadicam is a camera attached to a gyroscope. He walked all over Muir Woods National Park, filming. Instead of the normal speed of film that is 24 frames per second, he filmed one frame per second. When projected on the screen, it would give the illusion that the bikes traveled at an incredible speed. So, the speeder bike didn't actually hover or exist in real life on the planet Earth. I want a real speeder bike that hovers at that speed!

# Chapter Eighteen
## I'll Be in My Trailer!

THE NIGHT BEFORE our official first day on set, the lights were out early. No cards were being dealt and the basketball court was desolate. Our call times were before sunrise. All was quiet and still, but it was very hard to sleep that night.

We awoke to a damp, cold morning and lined up like school children waiting for our yellow bus. You could see our breath. Tommy opened the door and greeted us as we loaded in. Some of the really little Little People would climb up the steps into the bus on all fours because of their short inseams. They looked like rock climbers in Yosemite. This brought me back to when I was a young kid and my brothers would help me. I remember standing up on the seat in the station wagon while my parents drove us so I could see out the window. This was before child seats and seatbelt laws. I was now the big brother amongst the Little People and we all helped each other. We were in this together. We were a team.

The yellow bus rode so much differently on the dirt road. Where was the van from the other day? The yellow bus was meant to chauffeur children to school on a paved road; it obviously was not built for off-roading. As it swayed back and forth, we slid off the bench seats— our feet couldn't touch the ground to stabilize us. It was a stunt just riding on the bus!

As we continued down the dirt road, it shrunk and the trees crept in, their branches scraping against the windows. The bus maneuvered around 90-degree hairpin turns. The sheer drop off on one side was frightening to look down on. I could help but wonder, *Were we in good hands with Tommy our driver?* I hoped so.

We got off the bus and thanked God that no one had gotten carsick. I went to find my trailer. I was on contract and the #2 stuntman on the #1 movie of the year. I was feeling pretty great. When I couldn't find it, I asked the P.A. (production assistant) to point me in the right direction. He led me over to a large trailer and told me I'd be sharing it with eleven other men. *Gulp!* I thought I would have my own trailer. But there was no room in this forest for that and I needed my wardrobe assistants to help me dress into my costume. That let some of the air out of my balloon. I reminded myself that we were all in this together and we were on the same team. I threw my bag in the large trailer with eleven other bags and headed over to get breakfast. I made a note to myself, when I got back to Los Angeles I needed to sign with an agent!

It is typical when you are on location shooting a film, a caterer is hired to feed the entire cast and crew for breakfast, lunch, and/or dinner, depending on the hours worked. We were in the forest with no restaurants or commissary. Usually the food is really good and ready and hot for at least one-hundred-fifty people at the same time. Tables and chairs are set up under shelter for weather conditions. Some go as far as tablecloths, centerpieces, and fine china. The caterers hired were locals who most likely had never worked on a film before. They were unprepared and hit hard by one-hundred-fifty people. The food was good, but we were greeted with a new catering company the next day. It was not an easy job.

After breakfast, it was time to go back to the large trailer to dress. I knew it would be in my best interest to go to the bathroom before I suited up. The bathrooms were port-a-potties out in the wilderness, and you always wanted to be the first one to drop a deuce before anyone else. Kind of like a cat in a shared litter box. The cats race to go first.

In our trailer of twelve, we were put into sets of three people. The three of us shared a team of wardrobe assistants to help us dress and undress. I was happy to find Mike in my group of three. We would help each other out to give the assistants a little more time with the third guy in our group. He was smaller than us and more difficult to dress. Imagine stuffing a toddler into layers of snowsuits. Not easy. Each of us had a pair of baby blue pajamas that we wore under our foam fat suits. First day and I was already feeling a little self-conscious. I was a stuntman and I rode on a yellow school bus and now I was wearing baby blue pajamas. My manhood was taking a beating!

I found out that the wardrobe ladies were locals who lived in the area. They were not union wardrobe ladies. They were very professional, though. They were there every morning with a smile on their faces. Some of the littler Ewok extras had a harder time getting into their costumes, so this was a challenge. The ladies had to work extra hard to help the less agile Little People put on their costumes as well. At lunch and throughout the day, they would remove the heads and get us water. They kept an eye on us as best they could. Many times, they would lose us in the forest brush because of the height of the brush.

Many of the local people worked seasonal jobs and were happy to get on the crew. Out-of-work lumberjacks filled the need for extras portraying stormtroopers and rebel fighters.

The first scene up for the Ewoks in the U.S. was the discovery scene, where Luke, Han, Chewbacca, R2D2, and C3PO are captured. While the actors were in the net, they filmed their close-ups. Then they were switched out and their stunt doubles climbed back into the net. However, the actors were twisted with arms up and legs over each other in the net, so the stunt doubles had to mimic them precisely. It had to match exactly so that the audience could not tell the difference between the actors and the stunt doubles.

R2D2 cut the net so that the stunt doubles fell to the ground. The camera shot was so wide that the ground was shown. There were no crash pads for the stuntmen to land on and I think R2D2 landed on someone, too. R2D2's stunt double was an empty shell. The actors then switched back in and assumed the positions that the doubles ended up in.

The scene continued. In this particular scene, Kenny Baker, who was normally R2D2, was suited up as an Ewok. The English Ewok actors now had the bulk of the scene. Richard, the director, randomly selected twenty Ewoks to join. We lined up in full costume like a military inspection. Richard went down the line and pointed to the Ewoks he wanted. It was going to be a big extra scene and I, the stuntman was picked. I was now an extra. Argh! I didn't want to be an extra! I was a stunt guy! I was here to do stunts!

The other stunt guys were not picked so they undressed and trained some more. I knew those guys were hot on my trail, trying to be the better stuntman. We all had learned new tricks. I didn't want to fall behind. I trudged off and tried to find a place to hide in the scene. It was weird; I had been hoping forever to be in the *Star Wars* movies and here was my first shot and I wasn't very happy. I wanted to be working on my stunt skills. I didn't want to be an extra in the bushes.

On the first take, I guess my negative attitude was apparent. I was called out by the director, "Cut, you there!" Richard pointed at me, "You look rather bored."

My body language spoke volumes. I was not in the scene, I was out to lunch, dreaming of impressing my friends with my stunt skills. I thought, *What a great way to start*, and said, "Sorry sir, it won't happen again."

I was on camera standing right behind Harrison Ford in the scene and I knew better. The rest of the day I stayed in character. I did not think about stunts. A couple of hours later I finished the scene. The rest of the Ewoks gave me a hard time, "Way to break the ice Kev, glad it was you and not me." I deserved it!

As we took our Ewok heads off, breathing never felt so good! We hadn't even moved much, but we were soaking wet. The wardrobe assistants unzipped our backs and the cool air came in. Ah!

But there was no time to rest. I heard my name over the walkie talkie, "We need Kevin and Felix over by the clearing."

Yes!

Stunt time!

They were setting up a shot where the Ewoks were helping the rebels battle against the stormtroopers. I was to get wounded by a stormtrooper and fall to the ground. Most rehearsals were done without the Ewok heads on so we could get familiar with the area. When we rehearsed this scene, I performed the gag and accidently landed on a buried stump. I must have shown a grimace of pain because J.R. asked me what was wrong. I told him that I landed on something. He scolded me like a father, "You need to always check your landing area; your life may depend on it."

I learned the hard way and would now forever check my landing area. The rest of the day went fine, but that was not the start I was hoping for. We wrapped our first day and loaded the yellow school bus for home. Our bodies were sore. I reflected on the lessons learned. I would do better. I would make J.R. proud as if he were my father.

# Chapter Nineteen
## Team Work

O N THE SECOND day, every Ewok had to get dressed to shoot one big scene together. The Ewoks were to hide behind ferns that were at least six-feet tall. The tallest Ewok was four-foot-six.

"Greens Men" were crewmembers responsible for all the foliage and trees on set—things that were naturally in the forest. There were many ferns and they were constantly being replaced because when a shot was set up with electrical cables and lights, the crew tended to accidentally trample and squish the ferns. Every set up needed to be as fresh and identical to the shot before. The Greens Men officially earned the nickname, "The Fern Brothers."

When the time came, we were placed on set like a choreographed dance with our costumes and heads on. The director wanted to make sure to completely hide us with our heads on so that the ears wouldn't peak above the ferns. We were to hold bows and when he called "Action," we would all come out and shoot our arrows toward the camera simultaneously. When we rehearsed the scene the Ewoks couldn't be seen because they were still hidden—there was too much foliage and ferns!

So, we needed to start over, strategically replacing the ferns so not to hide the Ewoks *too* much. This took another fifteen minutes. Everyone was getting hot in the pre-roll drama.

Our Ewok eyes were now fogged up so we couldn't see. Our

latex gloves were tested as we tried to hold the arrow and bow. The temperature inside the costumes rapidly rose and someone yelled, "I need air." Many of the heads were not made to get oxygen as easily as others because of the design of the mouths. Some mouths were closed to have various looks. Those people would start breathing their own $CO_2$ instead of fresh oxygen. We would hear a *THUMP*! Ewok down! If an Ewok falls in the forest and no one is there, does it make a sound? It does!

When we paused to take a break, we were all antsy for those heads to come off. Production didn't want us to remove them because of the time involved. It took fifteen minutes to take off and another fifteen minutes to put it back on. We quickly learned that we wanted to be the first guy to get the head off and the last guy to get the head back on. This became a political game and was even kind of childish. Ewoks gone bad! Some even needed a time out. I couldn't play that game as a stuntman.

So, we tried again with the ferns. We were placed, hidden, heads on, loaded up with a bow and arrows. With the latex glove hands, you couldn't feel the arrows you were holding. The Ewok next to me dropped his and I heard muttering and moving about. We were getting ready to roll and I didn't want more drama, I just wanted the shot done. Our eyes had already fogged up and it was getting hot again. We both patted the ground for the arrow. It reminded me of looking for that lost quarter on the sticky ground in a dark movie theatre. I found the arrow for my friend just as the director yelled, "Rolling!" We got back into our hiding spots and I heard the follow-up call, "Action!"

We both stood and let our arrows fly. "Cut, great, moving on." Whew. We'd done it! We continued filming other arrow shooting scenes all day. Once everything was cut together it would look like a huge army of Ewoks. A group of thirty extras and stuntmen would appear to be hundreds.

Whenever there was a break in the action, I was able to have my head taken off and drink some much-needed water. I wanted to drink a gallon of it, but that would lead to me having to go to the bathroom. And if that happened, it shut down production because then *everyone* wanted to go. Restrooms were not close and we could not just make like a bear and tinkle near a tree or local bush. We would have to get out of costume, commandeer a jeep, travel down the mountain to the local porta-potty, and then wait for everyone to go. Of course, once everyone had a turn, we'd have to do everything again, in reverse.

Potty breaks took about half an hour! Production didn't like that. I didn't like having to put back on my wet, smelly costume. Have you ever put on old sweaty socks and underwear? Not wet from a pool. Sweaty wet, sticky, stinky sometimes with a thorn stuck in there somewhere. That type of wet. It was not fun.

We Ewoks were all brothers, trying to survive the conditions. I don't think anyone realized how hot it would be in the costumes, and with the restricted airflow, it made it even more difficult. Everyone worked hard every day. We needed to help each other when we could. Many times an Ewok would fall backwards. It was impossible for us to get back up on our own; it was like a turtle stuck on its back. It was funny because we could not see really each other with our giant furry heads on, so we would listen and search for the fallen Ewok and help them up. It was actually a beautiful thing.

# Chapter Twenty
## Stormtroopers

BULLDOGGING IS A term used in the rodeo. It refers to when a bulldog wrestles down a running steer by jumping and hanging on by its teeth. We, the stunt Ewoks, were about to perform our own version. Hopefully, no one was about to get bitten.

The stunt stormtroopers, were to be surprised by the attacking Ewoks as we jumped onto them from a log. It sounded simple enough: Felix, Michael, Chris and I were to appear and jump off a giant fallen redwood tree. We were in our stunt outfits but Richard thought we looked too thin. He requested full padding so we all hopped in a couple of jeeps and headed to our dressing trailer.

Our wardrobe ladies travelled with us and I was one of the lucky ones that day - I was in the first jeep. It kicked up all sorts of dust behind us. I could hear Felix and the rest of the guys complaining and couldn't help but laugh. I knew sooner or later I'd be the one eating dirt in the back. Throughout the day, a water truck sprayed the dirt roads to keep the dust down, but at the moment, it was bone dry.

Inside our trailers, we stripped out of our pads and suited up into the full padding. We kept our costume heads in our hands and jumped back into the waiting jeeps. I felt like I was in the army going to the front lines. Well, like a pretend army, without live ammunition or enemies trying to kill me. We headed back to the set and I was now in the rear jeep . . . breathing dirt and dust. Where was that water truck? Karma, baby, and now it was my turn. Who was laughing now?

When we arrived to the set, we rolled out of the jeeps like wine barrels. We struggled to climb onto the fallen tree. The crew had made a ramp and we were to run and jump off of it. The ramp helped us get some distance and speed for jumping.

The stunt guys set up pads so that we could land on them when we jumped off the fallen tree. We rehearsed a few times. The stunt guys moved the pads and stood in place of them, precisely where we are supposed to land. The director decided to roll film. We all suited up and got our heads on. The eyes in the head start fogging up and we all just had to deal with it. We got into place just off camera. It was that time… "Action!"

We all leapt to attack our designated stormtrooper and . . . missed, landing in a heap on the ground like a pile of poo—completely missing our target. My feet and legs stung. We Ewoks had developed a new language together. The harder and more uncomfortable we got, the Ewok muttering (complete with a few made up Ewok swear words) evolved. I had to walk it off. I did so with Ewok muttering, the new pig Latin, "O Jinks Wa Zee Ma." I had a feeling we were going to rehearse another dozen times.

The placement of the Ewoks and stormtrooper stunt guys was off. Apparently the stormtrooper's eyesight through their costumes was just as bad as ours. They snickered saying how they felt us go by. They just couldn't see us.

Every day was a learning process. We all had our heads removed and looked at each other's placement. We were off by just a few inches. We looked at our targets from our perch atop the fallen tree. I gauged the distance I would have to jump to reach my stunt guy. I wanted to land on him, not the ground again. We scampered down the ramp to get our heads on. I practiced running up the ramp in my full costume. I counted four steps as I ran to the edge. I waddled down the ramp to my starting spot. I was ready to do it again. "Action," was called and I tried to run up the ramp as fast I could. I felt like I was moving in slow motion. I jumped and . . . hit my intended target!

I heard a grunt. My stunt guy and I fell to the ground and started rolling. When we finally stopped, I was sitting on him. Tony, Felix, Michael, and Chris all crashed into their stormtroopers. It was organized chaos. And it was always a good thing especially when no one got hurt.

The stormtroopers were all surprised—we were much heavier than they thought we'd be. "I felt like I got hit by a bowling ball," one of them muttered.

Richard wanted one more take for safety, so we did it three more times (okay, maybe a dozen). Technical glitches caused the extra takes. But it was all in a day's work. We finished up and headed back to the dressing room to change out of our sweat-drenched costumes.

# Chapter Twenty-One
# Cary Grant and the Snorkel Lift

WHILE RIDING ON the bus back to the motel, I realized I was feeling a little homesick. One of my best friends was getting married and I was going to miss the wedding. I had a great excuse, but I wanted to be sure to let him and his bride know I was thinking about them. I considered flowers, but this wasn't a funeral. After some thought, I decided to send a telegram. It sounded so retro, so Cary Grant, and now that I was in the big time movies, I could be suave like Mr. Grant. "Dear Mr. & Mrs. Evans *stop* Congratulations *stop*"—you get the picture.

They told me that when they were walking out of the church being announced as Mr. and Mrs. Bryan Evans they received their telegram. It couldn't have been any more perfect for a more perfect couple. They still talk about it to this day. It's just one of those things, when you are on location and working six days a week, fourteen hours a day, you forget that there is life out there, away from the world of movies and make believe. I was feeling pretty good so I went over to the florist shop. I sent flowers to my mom and grandmother, tapping in once again to my inner Cary Grant. I just needed a scarf, a cigar, and a martini.

The day of the wedding I was sitting on top of a stationary Imperial walker. That was the only Imperial walker that was captured by Chewbacca. All the other ones were blown up. My job as an Ewok was to guard the captured stormtroopers on top of the walker. It was twenty-eight feet tall and made out of wood. I was the only Ewok up there for the scene.

I suited up and rode a snorkel lift to the top of the walker. The wardrobe assistant and prop master rode with me to put on the Ewok head and give me an Imperial blaster gun. Then they disappeared down the snorkel lift, leaving me alone.

I ended up staying up there for over an hour, waiting for the shot to be set up. As I sat, I learned how to tilt the head slightly so I could get air and look out from underneath the chin of the head. I had to be careful that the head didn't go too far back and fall, and of course, keep my balance so I didn't tumble off the walker! But most memorable of all, was the view and the feeling of being on that walker. There I was, looking down on giant trees, enjoying the peace and stillness of the forest from high above. A bird flew by, leading my eyes to the sky—I could see nothing but trees, all the way to the horizon. It was a beautiful sight that I'll never forget.

They rolled the cameras and yelled, "cut," "beautiful," and "check the gate." The scene didn't make it into the final cut; they ended up replacing me with Chewie on top of the walker. It made more sense for the storyline. But I was the only Ewok that got to see that view. It is one of my coolest memories.

The term "check the gate" means that once a scene is shot, the camera assistant opens the side of the camera to see if there are any fragments called "hairs" on the film. Those hairs ruin the shot with black streaks, so they have to check the gate before they move on to the next scene. So much time and money go into every single scene from set-up to break down. It takes a lot of people to make it happen.

# Chapter Twenty-Two
## Bad Seed

JUST LIKE BACK in school, there is always that guy. You know the type. He's not a team player. Everything revolves around him. We constantly have to wait for him. His needs are far more important than anyone else's. He always needs water, he needs a break, he's always more hot, tired, and uncomfortable than *everyone* else.

Most of us knew this guy from working with him on other films and he had a history of torpedoing projects and sapping group spirit. I had worked with him on *Under the Rainbow* and he hadn't changed a bit. He wouldn't listen to the choreographer, didn't follow directions, and was always quick to bark out his own set of orders every chance he got. He had even found a way to remove his costume head himself and would repeatedly do so during shots, thinking he was out of frame. But he would be *in* frame and we would have to repeat the scene, all because of him. Not to mention, he was a risk. Every move counts with stunt work, and mistakes can mean life or death. You don't want someone around who has a habit of failing to follow directions.

As hard as the rest of us worked, this guy made us look bad with all his phantom injuries, laziness, and mistakes. To make matters even worse, any scene he wasn't in, he'd brag about how he could have done it better! His bad attitude and lack of team spirit began to infect the rest of us and just as he did on other jobs, he was bringing the team down.

We all mentioned our long list of issues to production but they were too concerned about losing a body and being tasked with replacing it to do anything. So, they did nothing.

But someone had to do something.

I elected myself. I was a leader now. I needed to get rid of the bad apple before he spoiled the bunch. I know, I am a fine Catholic boy, and Father Murphy would not have seen it my way. Close your eyes Father, for I have sinned.

He had been torturing us long enough so I decided it was time to make *his* life a living hell. Of course, he loved taking his sweet time in the porta-potty. He always decided to go when we were all called to get dressed. Then he would stay in there for a long time and miss the scene. Batter up! That day, we were called to get dressed, and like clockwork, he headed to the porta-potty.

Well, it was time for him to get a dose of his own. He closed the door and I rolled a big rock in front of it so he couldn't get out. I then started throwing rocks at the porta-potty. Felix and Chris caught me. I told them who was in there. They looked at me and smiled with devilish grins. Oh, Father Murphy, you'd better put them on your prayer list, too! They picked up a few rocks and started throwing them at the porta-potty too. The echo could be deafening inside of that portable plastic hut. We all tried to keep from laughing as we went to get in costume.

As I walked to my dressing room, I heard him trying to get out. He couldn't. He was stuck for a while and as the day got warm, the stinkier it got. The stinky Ewok got stinkier. No one was around to help him because everyone else was actually working. We made a point to do this routine every time he went to do his whole hide-in-the-porta-potty-to-get-out-of-work-thing.

It was our little secret. He started looking around to see if anyone was watching him. We were very stealthy about it. As soon as he went in, we would go to work. One of us would roll a rock to block the door. Production would have to let him out. He complained to Dave and Bill about it. And to this day, I don't know if they knew it was us. They never said. It only took a few days and the bad seed decided to take the next airplane home.

Once he was gone, we were a much happier crew. I know it sounds merciless, but we needed to work together as a happy unit.

# Chapter Twenty-Three
## The Battle

J.R. SET UP a scene. Five of us stunt Ewoks were to sneak up and attack three stunt stormtroopers while they shot their weapons at three other Ewoks running by. We all rehearsed without our heads on. It was a series of beats, like a dance number. Each of us had a designated stormtrooper that we were to hit on the head with a club and wrestle to the ground. The rehearsal was to give the camera, director, actors and all involved a chance to see the actual scene and work out any glitches.

When we were ready, we placed our heads on and prepared to shoot.

"Action!" We sneaked up and attacked the stormtroopers. We hit them, but they didn't fall. The director yelled, "Cut!" and asked what happened. Why hadn't the stormtroopers fallen? They said they were waiting for the Ewoks to hit them. They couldn't feel us! My designated stormtrooper took my prop club and started hitting his own arm with it. He told us we really had to hit them hard and not to worry about hurting them because the club was made out of balsa wood, which is very light.

So, we got ready to go again. We attacked, swinging our clubs with all our might, and down they went! We did a victory dance and ran off.

The director yelled, "Cut!" and "Moving on." Then he added, "That was great."

I took my head off and looked down at my stormtrooper, still on the ground. He looked up at me wearing an expression of shock and awe. "Wow you guys can hit hard," he said, impressed.

After making sure he was okay, we gave our clubs back to the prop master. "I didn't know you were going to actually hit them," he said with a chuckle. "Those were real clubs. You guys really clocked them!"

Apparently, he hadn't heard the conversation, but he realized the stormtroopers didn't feel the hits and had switched out the clubs. Unbeknownst to all of us, they were not balsa wood clubs anymore. The stunt stormtroopers didn't complain, but now they knew we could hit.

The next day we started rehearsing the big battle with the stormtroopers. The stunt Ewoks would start by either swinging in on ropes or flying off the Russian swing. Michael and Chris were chosen for the Russian swing. Felix and I would be on the ropes. We rehearsed with the big stunt pads first so that we knew where to place the stunt stormtroopers. Bob Yerkes was guiding the swing. Chris and Michael would fly off the swing onto two unsuspecting stormtroopers. Felix and I would swing in on ropes taking out two more stormtroopers. The other Ewoks would then descend into the scene, once again making it seem like there were hundreds of Ewoks rather than thirty. That is what we all hoped for. We rehearsed this scene over and over again all morning until it was right and we all had our choreographed timings down.

We left the area to change into our costumes and the Greens Men came in with fresh foliage, trees, and lush greenery, making it look like no one had been there. Every detail was tended to—they even raked the dirt so there were no footsteps. We were all dressed and excited to get this big scene started after rehearsing all morning. The director decided to just go for it and roll on the first take.

Everyone went to their start marks. Felix and I were on a fallen tree log ready to swing in. Bob started the swinging motion to get to the desired height on the Russian swing for Chris and Michael. Bob gave the signal and "Action," was called. The stunt stormtroopers ran into the scene, Michael and Chris flew off the swing a little high and hit the stormtroopers on the head rather than the chest. They all went down harder than we had rehearsed. Felix and I swung in and missed our stormtrooper. *Where the heck were they?* I thought. This wasn't looking like the scene from that morning.

It continued from bad to worse when suddenly the rest of the thirty Ewoks all came rushing in and ran into each other. I couldn't help but think of Larry, Curly and Moe. "Cut!" was yelled loud and clear.

After that debacle, the crew realized the problem, and not to point fingers, but the marks were moved due to making the scenery look lush and untouched. The marks were accidently touched all right, leaving many of us with bumps and bruises.

Production had a big problem because no one could see. Ewok and stormtrooper costumes had terrible eyesight. We lost our bearings with our heads on. The eyes in the Ewok head fogged up. The eyes on the stormtrooper head distorted the depth of field. Getting to our marks was tough for all of us. From anti-fog Windex to tiny air holes, we had tried different ways to address the eyeball problem, but nothing seemed to work.

The stunt guys made the necessary adjustments and it was on to take two. The set-up of the shot had taken too much time already. If every Ewok and stormtrooper took off their head, it was going to be a long wait.

We were given numbers so that instead of "Action," the director would yell out, "Ewok one" for the Ewok's action for that desired moment. It went on with "Ewok two" and "Ewok three." That way, there was not too much confusion with each beat of action. The scene was still chaotic, but it was a little more organized chaos.

We were all so tired. One time there were two Ewoks that ran into each other by accident and the next thing we knew, they started fighting. Punches were thrown, arms were flying, and legs were kicking. It was funny because they couldn't see, and when they were trying to hit each other they would miss like little old drunk men walking home from the local tavern. I never saw the outtakes from this but I imagine it was hilarious for the crew to watch. We all calmed down and we continued the shot again and again from many different angles. When the scene was over, we cheered.

The long days of shooting took their toll. Many Ewok actors had aches and pains as we waited for our yellow school bus. That was how a legend was born. Warwick was not cast as Wicket initially. He was an extra. His charm and exuberance brought him a lot of attention and the mere fact that he was, and acted like, a child. They decided to pull a few strings to bring him to America. He would play an Ewok child. I think they saw something in him and knew a role was going to pop up for him. It did, in the most Hollywood of moments.

Kenny Baker was cast as Wicket. And on the day of his big scene with Princess Leia, he fell ill. Oh, what to do? It was Carrie Fisher's last day on set. Tomorrow she was to fly to San Francisco to start filming at ILM. The whole day was devoted to that one scene. The First Assistant Director, David Tomlinson, said, "Let's try Warwick. If the scene doesn't work, Kenny will be better tomorrow." The production team all looked at each other and decided that was the best plan. If it didn't work Carrie would just fly a day later.

Warwick accepted the challenge. Carrie agreed, too. Warwick hit it out of the park. His energy and child wonderment captured the hearts of the production team. He was a child and played it like a child. Kenny, being a man, would have played the scene differently. I am not saying one was better than the other, but Warwick's portrayal was perfect. To Kenny's credit, I never heard a negative word from him. He was happy for Warwick and still is to this day.

Everyone looked forward to pay day after working a long week. The accountants came every Thursday to hand deliver checks to the cast and crew. The Ewok extras looked at their checks and seemed really disappointed—almost mad. They were expecting overtime pay for the long hours they worked each day. I hadn't noticed any discrepancies in my check, because I was on a union contract, but I did notice their attitude and that affected me. They asked Dave and Bill who told them it was just an accounting error, "Don't worry. We will check it out." Dave and Bill came back to tell the non-union Ewoks that production had said there was no error.

The non-union Ewoks had signed on that their rate was per day and per day was not always eight hours. It varied and was however many hours necessary each day. The Ewok family was not happy but production was not budging. I think production thought they had the Ewoks by the tail—if Ewoks had a tail. Many of them had quit their regular jobs to get this once in a lifetime opportunity, but no one liked to be taken advantage of. They had worked so hard for so little and we needed a plan.

The ride in our yellow school bus home was quiet and Tommy our driver knew something was up. We started talking to him about our dilemma. For the next few days, we continued working without much excitement. We dressed a little more slowly and no one jumped at the chance to get into more scenes. The week wore on as production tried to finish up with the main cast to get them down to ILM. We would then have three weeks of second unit shots with just Ewoks. Production was pushing us hard and there was a lot to do in a short amount of time. Our Ewok heads were not being taken off as frequently because production thought it was taking too much time. We were exhausted and pissed. We called it a night and went to bed early.

# Chapter Twenty-Four
# Revenge of the Ewoks

T HE STUNT EWOKS' call time was a half hour earlier than the extra Ewoks. We were picked up in a van instead of the yellow school bus. Other than that, it was like any other morning. The yellow school bus arrived with Dave and Bill, who were constantly with us from the audition to the final wrap of the movie. They got off the bus with a peculiar look on their faces. Production greeted the bus like every other day to help the Little People off the bus, but to their surprise, there were no Little People on the bus.

Dave and Bill told production that the extra Ewoks had had enough. They were working too hard, the heads were kept on too long, and they weren't getting paid for overtime. Their contracts were per day and they were unenforceable, so they didn't need to stick around. He explained that the extra Little People were at the airport going home. The production laughed it off and thought they were joking so they climbed onto the bus and looked around—even under the seats. The bus was empty. Tommy the driver didn't know what to say. We watched all this commotion. There was a lot of panic and yelling. Everyone blamed each other. The production would have to be shut down without the extra Ewoks. George Lucas and Richard Marquand were back at ILM with the rest of the cast. We were left behind with the second unit to finish up all the Ewok scenes.

We heard the first assistant director tell a production assistant to get on the yellow school bus and tell the Ewoks at the airport that their demands would be met. Tommy and the production assistant were about to leave, when all of a sudden, the doors of the wardrobe trailers flew open and out came all the extra Ewoks! They were hootin' and hollerin' with T-shirts that said, "Revenge of the Ewoks." Production was had. The Ewoks made a stance to better their working conditions. All of us, who had the earlier call to be on set, had been in on it and totally supported our Ewok family.

Revenge of the Ewoks took a lot of work and thought to pull it off. All of the extra Ewoks got up extremely early and met Tommy and the yellow bus to take them to the set before anyone else got there. Tommy had the keys to the wardrobe trailers to let the Ewoks in. They hid behind their own Ewok costumes that were hung up every night. They had to be really quiet, because the wardrobe department didn't even know they were there. Then Tommy had to go back to the hotel and pick up Dave and Bill so that they would arrive with an empty bus at the regular extra Ewoks' call time. Thank goodness the stunt Ewoks happened to have an earlier call time to be on set and that was why a van had been sent for us. While this planning was being done, complete secrecy was accomplished. We never gave away our Teamster driver. Everyone knew who helped us. There was no way to prove that Tommy had helped us and he was never fired. The production team had a very good, but nervous laugh. The crew had a good laugh, too. It was these moments that brought everyone together with unity. The crew and Ewoks had a skip in their step and we actually got a lot of work done that day.

This was a great win for the extra Ewoks. J.R. though, came up and told us they all deserved the extra special treatment. We did not. We were stuntmen and now we would have to work harder to get everything done. "Let them have their breaks," he said. "You, my friends, will not."

# Chapter Twenty-Five
## Explosions

I WAS EXCITED TO work on the next scene. There was a large catapult sitting in the forest. I walked around the machine to check out how talented and crafty Ewoks were to build such a contraption. I was proud of myself and the tribe! This demonstrated that we were more like primitive man than animal. The construction and engineering required to build them meant we had complex brains. The Ewoks would use the catapult to fire on their enemy, the Imperial walkers.

As the walker came into range, we were to launch our rocks. Chris was the spotter, and he directed us where to aim. Michael and I were the two Ewoks that would load the rocks onto the catapult. Three other Ewoks would crank the arm of the catapult so that it would fire. In the movie it would look like our catapult hurled giant rocks hundreds of feet. The reality was the rocks weighed about one pound and were made of Styrofoam. They only traveled ten feet with a strong wind behind them. It took a lot of imagination on our parts.

We set up the scene with all of us at the catapult. The crank of the arm was the only real thing that worked. We pulled the arm back to cock it, and then used a clip to keep it pulled back. Then Michael and I would load the rock. We simulated the weight of the rock to make it appear really heavy. Michael and I rehearsed our routine to lift and set the rock in the cup of the arm. We moved the catapult slightly. The dang thing was heavy. Chris signaled us to fire. Michael and I pulled the clip out to release the arm.

The rock flew, in our minds, hundreds of feet. Once again, I was playing in my back yard. My imagination went crazy. There were no real Imperial walkers, but in my imagination, they were everywhere. We had to destroy them.

As the rock flew, we had to track it with our eyes. We did this by counting in our heads like we did for a dance step. With our heads on, through those nasty plastic eyes, all we could see were shadows, but you already knew that. With our heads off, we could see that there was a row of trees. They became our landmarks. Once our heads were on, we could see the shadows of the trees, therefore making it easier to focus in the direction of the trees as a unit. It made it look like all of us were watching the rocks sail in the air at the same time. The director would count and we would imagine the projection of the rock. He would then say "hit" or "miss" and we'd react, then go back to loading and shooting. I lost myself in the scene. Then all of a sudden, the director would yell, "The walker sees you. Run!!"

I would get excited; my heart pumping and I would run super-fast. Then a flash of small fire explosions went off around the catapult. They were called squibs. We knew where they were placed and approximately when they would go off. It was easy to react because it was loud and we could see the brightness of the flame. I reacted like it was real because, in actuality, there still was a chance that our Ewok fur could catch on fire by a rogue spark. Ewok fur smelled terrible when it burned. I ran away like my life depended on it. I think I ran into Michael one time, maybe more. I would feel a big thunk and then hear a noise like a football player being tackled. Uff! Heck, we couldn't see much.

Squibs were used for blasts of small explosions. Mortars were used for large explosions. Those could be dangerous. The mortar was a five-inch-wide tube by six-inches long. It was packed with black gunpowder, dirt, and small rocks. The special effects man had a wooden box that was wired to synchronize the effects with a push of a button for each explosion. Our lives were in his hands. At times, they even blew up trees. Large pieces of the tree would fly in my direction. Some of these pieces were over ten feet long. I had no idea until I took my head off, then I would look by my feet and somehow there would be these pieces lying next to me. Many times, the battle was a little too real.

# Chapter Twenty-Six
# Greens Men: Friends or Foe

I LEARNED ABOUT WIDOWMAKERS from the Greens Men while filming in the forest. They were a real threat that would stop production. Widowmakers are dead branches, detached from the tree, that hang precariously from live branches. Sometimes, these widowmakers are as large as a tree itself and can fall if gravity or the wind pulls them down. And in Endor, the trees were all huge. Widowmakers were no joke.

As we moved around the set, the Greens Men would keep a keen eye for widowmakers. If someone was below and a branch fell on them, they could be killed. Hence the name, "widowmaker." If they became a threat, the Greens Men would get a snorkel lift, go into the trees, and remove it. We would get to take a break and get a breath of fresh air.

Being outside in a forest, all of the Ewok exterior shots required a lot of maintenance. The Greens Men had to keep all the elements of the forest looking fresh and untouched. From the trees, ferns, and grass to the rocks, dirt, and even the bugs, they made everything look perfectly magical regardless of how many people had trampled through. It had to look pristine and they worked very hard to keep it that way. I really admired them, but would soon develop a love-hate relationship.

Dwarf bodies really aren't built like Olympic athlete Jessie Owens, but for some reason, our choreographer wanted us to run like Jessie. Our little inseams and the thickness of the foam would not allow us to bring our knees up close to our chests and run. It looked as if the Ewoks were skipping. We had to learn to maneuver our legs every which way to get up over rocks, downed trees, stumps, and shrubs. Our littlest Ewoks had a hard time getting over the bugs and banana slugs. If one Ewok slipped on the moss, it would take out a whole line of Ewoks—like a bowling ball on an oiled lane.

We rehearsed our scene with our heads off, like we always did. When we rehearsed, we counted our steps so that we could stop and hit our marks, that way the camera would get its shot. We never ran in a perfect straight line; we had to zigzag and make it look nonchoreographed and chaotic because we are running from either stormtroopers or Imperial walkers. Everyone knew what to do and where to go. The crew and camera operators knew where to focus. We knew where the special effects department was going to set up each explosion and which Ewok had to fall to the ground like it had been hit. It was complicated and took a lot of patience.

During all the rehearsals we trampled the whole vegetation and had kicked up a lot of dirt. So, while we were getting suited up and ready for the shot, the Greens Men replaced everything with new plants, making it look perfect again. The wardrobe ladies lined us up on our start marks. I was to lead the pack running. Upon hearing, "Action," I took off while counting my steps and... *BAM*! I ran smack into a six-foot tall Fernus Gigantus. The Greens Men had placed it right in my path! It was so big that it stopped me in my tracks. The three guys behind me stacked up like an accordion until we shot backwards and all fell on top of each other.

We heard, "Cut!" and everyone watching busted up laughing.

Those of us on the ground were not laughing. We had no idea what had just happened—why had our carefully planned steps not worked? The wardrobe ladies took off our heads and we looked around to see this gigantic fern that had miraculously popped up! This was when I no longer loved our Greens Men. At that moment I hated them.

We had to start all over again with our heads off and counting steps. We fell a lot and looked like Keystone Cops. It was another very long day.

# Chapter Twenty-Seven
## Learning on the Fly

ACH AND EVERY shot of the film was drawn out on a shot sheet illustrated like a flip book that had been approved by George Lucas. The crew used this as a guide to set up each shot. I remember seeing the director of photography, also known as the cinematographer, Jim Glennon, examining the book and moving the camera around, trying to find the right shot that perfectly mimicked each drawing.

One particular afternoon was full of action work with Ewok extras. Action work is basically general chaos. Ewoks were running and hiding from stormtroopers and stormtroopers were running from attacking Ewoks. We all ran around until we got tired. As a stunt guy, I couldn't get tired. I had to keep running. Production was switching out Ewok extras after every take when they got tired, but we stunt guys had to keep our energy up. That was our job.

I heard my name crackle on the walkie-talkie. I was needed at another location ASAP.

I jumped into the jeep and headed to a new location in the forest for my next stunt. A huge seventy-foot crane sat at the edge of a cliff overlooking a valley of dead trees. I stared at it with butterflies in my stomach. The crane was for me. Gulp.

A couple stormtrooper stunt guys approached. They were out of costume and helping out with the scene. "Hey Kev, we're going to swing you in over this valley. Are you up for that?" I nodded. The cameramen from ILM came over to explain how it would work. I was to swing across the valley, pretend to land on a platform, then swing back. In the film, it would look like I was swinging into the village. This was a big stunt and I was proud to be asked to do it. In our two weeks in the forest, I had proven myself and they had chosen me to tackle it. But I'd be lying if I said I wasn't nervous. That crane was high!

During the shot, they would use Vista Vision cameras. These cameras have a higher resolution, wide screen variant of the 35mm motion picture film format cameras. George used them exclusively for special effect shots. The camera looked completely different—the film was threaded sideways instead of through the top. This gives a clearer and wider picture. I had studied these cameras in college and was excited to be filmed by them.

They told me the crane operator was the best one in the county. *Hm. Okay*, I thought. I wondered how many crane operators there were in this county, but no time for pondering, I had to accept it and prepare. I wanted to be *the* stunt guy. Here was my chance.

The scene was where the Ewoks catch the heroes, tie them up, and carry them through the village on poles. The camera pans the heroes and continues to me. I wave to my Ewok family and swing into the imaginary village. Just like the platform I'd pretend to land on, ILM would create the village in postproduction with special effects.

We first rehearsed with a sandbag. The prop guys attached the bag and my stunt buddy, let it fly. It soared across the valley. As it reached the end of the pendulum swing, my stunt buddy told me that was where I'd put my feet down, making it looked like I landed.

I watched the bag start swinging back on the return and was feeling pretty confident. My stunt team and I smiled at each other and nodded, all feeling great until… *PPFFFT!* The sand bag was impaled! The platform had wooden posts sharpened to points on the end to represent primitive architecture. My eyes went wide as I stared at my stand-in, hanging from the spike!

I looked over at one of my stunt buddies. He quickly diverted his eyes and looked to the crane operator. I looked to the crane operator. The crane operator didn't seem rattled. That made one of us! He nodded his head and held up a finger. He wanted another rehearsal. I did too! Gulp!

For the next rehearsal, the crane operator rotated the cab to extend the swing. At the end of the swing he rotated it back ever so slightly. This time the sand bag flew right between the posts, into my stunt buddy's arms. I looked at the crane operator. He had a satisfied look on his face and gave me a wink. I hoped that wasn't dust in his eye!

The stunt team told me that they didn't know how many times production was going to do this shot, so to be on the safe side they were going to put me in a harness. That meant I had to undress out of my costume, leaving me only in my baby blue pajamas.

Once down to my PJs, I stepped one leg at a time into the harness. The stunt team cinched it up tight and put a carabineer in so I could be attached to the rope. I put my costume back on and the wardrobe gal cut a little hole in my costume so the carabineer could be exposed. The rope that I would swing on was a cable dressed to look like a rope. With my stunt Ewok hands, it would definitely be a challenge to hang on.

The Ewoks set to carry the heroes, started making noise about how long they had to stand in their costumes. The camera department started hollering about losing sunlight. We needed to shoot ASAP. I was not even attached to the rope yet and everyone was telling each other we had to move immediately. All the chatter and hullabaloo just added to my nerves. I had to breathe.

Lucky for me, my stunt team was unfazed. They were focused and continued through the motions of keeping me safe. When the special effects guys finished rigging the rope, the stunt team hooked me up with a couple of carabineers. They told me not to worry about the sharp post. Our crane operator had seen what happened and fixed it. "Just do the action as you were told," they said.

I was still a little nervous, but I looked to the crane operator and gave him the thumbs up. He returned it and the wardrobe gal put my Ewok head on.

Everyone raced against the setting sun as the yelling and tension increased. The Ewoks with the photo doubles of the main actors suited up, and the poles were placed on their shoulders. "Action!"

I took a deep breath. The Ewoks started to walk. Someone fell. "Cut!"

The Ewoks had not rehearsed with their heads on. It was hard enough to walk in the Ewok costume, let alone carrying someone while walking in unison. Production and the wardrobe gals got the Ewoks back to their start marks. I stood on my mark with the rope in my hand. My heart was beating really fast. Waiting wasn't easy. I couldn't see anything because . . . yeah, you know—those Ewok eyes. It was like everything was covered in instant fog. I could feel my toes on the edge of the platform. I stepped back a little bit but I was tethered to the rope. All I could do was keep listening.

The camera department barked louder at production about the light. We started the scene late in the afternoon so the sunlight at dusk would give it a magical look. The only problem was everyone seemed to have forgotten what a huge production it would be getting about twelve Ewoks to carry a bunch of heavy photo doubles while another Ewok flew through the air on a rope. It sounded simple if you didn't think about all the logistics—well, maybe it didn't sound so simple. Everyone tends to believe their job is most important. My dear mother would be shouting, "My son's safety is most important!" I would have to agree.

One of the stunt team members came over and removed my head. He gave a little slack on the rope and asked, "How are you doing? Do you need anything?" I said no. I just wanted to do the stunt and stop thinking about it.

The wardrobe gals removed the Ewok heads of the other Ewoks and production got them back in line. I was thinking maybe they should have used dummies instead of photo doubles. It would have been much easier. All of a sudden, I heard a voice on the walkie-talkie say, "Do the prop people have any dummies for photo doubles?" I chuckled to myself.

Everyone was rushing around so fast they were not thinking clearly. I hoped my crane operator was thinking clearly. My life was literally in his hands. The prop guys now all rushed to the prop truck and fetched several dummies, even one that looked like Chewbacca.

Communication breakdown can halt a war or a movie. Wendy (our choreographer) taught the Ewoks how to walk in unison. She should have been there sooner. It was clear—this scene had turned into a bigger production than originally thought.

As I waited to do my stunt, thoughts of the many things that could go wrong invaded my mind. I had to push them away. The camera department was still yelling about losing light. Time was ticking away and everyone was feeling its pressure.

My stunt buddy, probably sensing my anxiety and terrible thoughts, came over and we went through everything. "Let the rope do the work," he said, staring me straight in the eye. "The crane operator will bring you safely home and I'll be here to catch you." He reminded me to stay calm and even, keeping a steady swing out and back.

We heard production say the Ewoks were ready and my wardrobe gal put my head on. With one more word of encouragement from my stunt buddy, the two left me on the platform. I waited for my cue, careful to not let the wind blow me away! I adjusted my footing and tried to relax.

# Chapter Twenty-Eight
## Finally

"ACTION!" YELLED THE director. I couldn't see them but guessed the Ewoks were marching with the dummies. "Wave, Kev!" he yelled. I waved. I put both hands on the rope and felt my feet leave the platform. I was hanging on and I was flying. It was a long pendulum swing. I felt the zenith of the swing and put my feet out to touch the imaginary platform on the other side of the valley. The swing ended and I started soaring back.

I was now in the hands of my crane operator. I remained calm. I felt the boom of the crane move slightly and realized that was what the operator had to do to give me a safe landing. I was completely in his hands. I couldn't help but wonder: *Would I be impaled? Would I fall into the dead orchard? Or would I safely land?*

My question was answered as my stunt buddy reeled me in. I hit him like a sack of potatoes and we both fell onto the platform. I jumped up and with my head still on I asked, "Did we get the shot?"

"No," I heard.

Ugh.

There was a problem. We would have to do it again. Back to our start marks, we went. All I had to do was turn around and *not* fall off the platform.

I tried not to think too much. Part of me felt even more nervous now that I had done it safely once. All I could think about was how everything could go wrong the second try. That swing back had to be tricky for my operator. *Was I lucky or was he that good? Could I do it again? Could we do it again?*

Production started barking that they were ready for another take. I imagined the Ewoks, all lined up. I didn't know because my head never came off. I was still tethered to the rope, a sweaty hot mess. I was asked if I was okay and I gave the thumbs up.

I heard production yell, "Rolling" and got ready. I took a deep breath. *Here we go again.*

"Action! . . . Wave, Kev," yelled the director. I waved and confidence started flowing through my body. This time I jumped more gracefully, as if I actually lived in the trees. I let out a Tarzan yell (that probably only I could hear) and took in the swing, fully enjoying the ride.

The swing out was a rush—that was the fun part. It was like my own personal rollercoaster. I could feel some of the wind blowing through my head—it was awesome. I started to feel my speed slow. The ride wasn't over but I put my legs out as if I were a bird landing on a tree branch.

I knew the swing back was out of my control. I reminded myself to relax. If my body were rigid, it would make for an easier target for the spike to stick me. If I pretended I was a big pillow, maybe I would bounce off the spike. I felt the boom arm gently swing. I sensed that I was on track toward the landing area. My life was in the crane operator's hands. I hoped to land on the platform.

Oh, I did. Like a wrecking ball.

I hit my stunt buddy so hard I knocked him flying. But he held onto me so I wouldn't fall off. Stuntmen are tough as nails. As we lay crumpled, we heard the director yell, "Cut, print, check the gate!"

We picked ourselves up and he unhooked me from the rope. My wardrobe lady removed my head. I immediately looked to the crane operator and gave him an enthusiastic thumbs up. We had done it. *Phew!*

We celebrated and once we got back down to the ground, I took a moment to feel it beneath my feet. Having conquered the crane, I felt incredible and ready for whatever came next.

.

# Chapter Twenty-Nine
## Home Away from Home

THE RIDE HOME on the bus was quiet for me. I didn't talk much. My feel-good high after the crane stunt was swiped when I received stunt pay for the swing and other stunts I did that day. I learned that if my work didn't make it into the film, I would not get paid.

The swing back was not on film.

The danger that came with the swing back, I didn't receive stunt pay for. I sat in the bus realizing that the most dangerous part of the stunt wasn't paid work. I was alive. That obviously mattered, but I couldn't help but feel a little bummed.

Every day was a learning experience. I learned many people got hurt when the camera stopped rolling. I was lucky.

Tony asked if I was going to play basketball. At first, I declined, but I knew I needed to get out of my funk and playing basketball could be just the thing to do it. So, after putting my bag in my room I headed over to where the guys were playing and joined in the game.

I took a moment to take in the whole motel life we were living. This was now our metropolis. I was playing the part as a school kid on the black top. There were the quiet ones who retreated to their rooms, the card players who played into the night, and even two sets of girl gangs who would talk about each other. One group was quiet and the other was loud. When the quiet ones were not around the loud ones would talk about each other. There were the smokers who would congregate at one end of the motel—Marty put an ashtray there for them. There were two married couples. One had two daughters, who were both Little People. The other was a mixed couple—he was little and she was of average height. He was in the movie and she was not. They had three boys. She stayed behind and watched the kids. They had the two big kitchenettes. Their rooms were right next to each other.

Warwick and his friend would come over and it was a regular playground. We all looked out for each other. We gave each other a hard time but it was all out of love. One day we had a huge water fight. We were all having fun drenching each other with squirt guns, buckets of water, and of course water balloons. It was epic. Everyone was soaking wet, smiles all around.

We had two bully incidents. One Tony took care of immediately. There was one little guy who was bigger than most of the other Little People, and he tried to throw his weight around. He started pushing everyone and then he pushed Tony. *Whap-whap-whap!* Tony smacked him three times before he knew what hit him. He was taken away by his friend and was a bully no more.

The other bully was taken care of by me. This one knucklehead was bullying a lot of smaller Ewok extras as well as the wardrobe ladies. People would complain to production but it fell on deaf ears. They did nothing and so this Ewok continued to ruin our happy unit.

On one particular day, I was out of costume, watching him rehearse while he was in costume, jumping off a rock. I decided that this was the time to set him straight. Right before he jumped, I knocked the wind out of him with a punch to his gut. As he doubled over, I spoke right into his ear, "Knock it off with the bullying, we have had enough." He went down like the coward he was. He wasn't a problem after that.

Like I said, we were a family and cared for each other. Sometimes there are family squabbles. Locals would come by, mostly out of curiosity. For the most part they left us alone. Sometimes we would cruise around town in one of the extra Ewok's cars. We went to a local pub for a beer. We would have fun just chatting up the locals. One of the barflies once asked if we were there for the show. "Show, what show?"

"Lil Butch is singing and yodeling tonight."

*Really?!* We all looked at each other. This couldn't be our Ewok, Butch. The guys were not really into country and western, especially yodeling. I tried to convince them to stay. "How many times are we going to be able to say we heard Butch sing?" I couldn't seem to convince them and we downed our drinks and headed for the door.

But just before we left the place, Butch came striding in. He had an entourage—two girls on each arm. Butch, in full cowboy getup, hat, boots, fringe, and a smile from ear to ear, eyed us and said, "You boys here to watch me sing?"

"Why yes, Butch, heck yeah, we're here to watch you sing. We may even listen a little, too."

We had no idea. Butch was a regular celebrity. I looked around and there were posters advertising his appearance. My buddies were still trying to leave, and they gave me glaring looks.

"Aren't you as intrigued as I am?" I asked. "We have been riding this bus for the last couple of weeks and I didn't know he sang. I know he's tough. Heck, he looks tough and rough like he has been in a few fights. He must have earned the name "Butch" somewhere."

It worked. They were in and we bellied back up to the bar. Somebody started buying us drinks. Butch started singing and people poured in. Before long, the place was packed! We didn't know any of his songs but we sang along with the other barflies.

We stumbled out of there at who knows what time. When we saw Butch the next time, we just smiled and yelled Lil' Butch. He smiled back. One of our fellow Ewoks was a small-town country legend and we loved it!

# Chapter Thirty
## Tug of War

THE NEXT DAY on the bus I sat next to the English actors and said, "I haven't seen you guys around." Like I mentioned before, the production had broken up into at least five different units. They might have been working but it hadn't been on the same location I was at.

They said that they had been working a lot less lately and that it was all up to their stuntmen to make them look good. That made me laugh. Warwick chimed in and said there was a big stunt that we were all supposed to do that day. We were going to trip one of the Imperial walkers. That sounded fun to me.

I hoped I would be in the scene and would have loved to ask, but I had already found out the hard way . . .do not ask J.R. what we're doing. Many times, I had no idea what I was about to film until I got to the set. I asked J.R. once what we were doing that day and he replied, "You will do whatever I tell you to do and be glad for it."

I never asked again.

J.R. earned my respect right away. He had a way of putting me in my place. I felt like that snot-nosed kid that asks a lot of questions, so I settled down. To be honest, I was that kid because all of this was new to me being twenty-two years old on the biggest production of the year.

Warwick seemed to get the scoop and I thought I should stick with him more often. He was going places. He reminded me of the little salesman that goes door to door in the 50's and sells household cleaners to all the stay-at-home housewives—except everybody liked him.

I got distracted on the bus. One of the guys started singing the words, "breakfast burrito," and nothing else. He put a space between each syllable. It sounded like "break-fast bur-ri-to." We were bored on this monotonous bus trip. It was funny. He stopped singing. Then someone dared him to sing all the way to the location. He accepted the challenge. The bus heard "break-fast bur-ri-to" for the next half an hour. I think I would have rather heard Butch yodeling again. We threw things at him; we tried to cover his mouth. Nothing worked. We were all thankful when we arrived. I don't think anybody ordered a breakfast burrito from catering that morning.

J.R. stopped the Ewok stunt guys and told us to put on our regular padding. "You'll thank me for it," he said. He smiled knowingly and walked away.

*What does he mean by that?* I wondered. I knew I couldn't ask him what we were going to do. We moseyed over to catering, had a bite, and then got dressed for the day.

They set up the first shot by two special trees. Yes, we were in a forest and there were a lot of trees, but these two were perfect for what we were going to do. Warwick was right. We were going to use a rope to trip the walker!

We rehearsed with our heads off, like we always did. The English Ewoks would be at the front to signal us to pull. Kenny, Chris, and Michael, were on one side. Felix, Tony, Warwick and I were on the other. We did a few set ups to get all the leads their close-ups. Warwick got his, too. Wardrobe came over and took off our heads and we got a little water break. J.R. and the stunt team came over and explained that we would be attached to the trip rope. J.R. said that we failed at trying to trip the walker. We all looked at each other.

"What do you mean?" asked Felix.

"Well that's a mechanical machine," said J.R. "If you guys tried to stop a car with that rope, what would happen?"

We all thought about that. "So, we don't stop it? Then what happens?"

"We're going to pull you for four seconds. Then you will all get up and we'll pull you again for four seconds. Always be counting to four. You will have four seconds to get up after we drag you."

"Why four?" someone asked.

"Think of the Imperial walkers. Their legs move every four seconds. You guys catch one of the walker's legs." He made a hand gesture to simulate the walker's legs as he counted to four.

I was thinking that some of these guys would take a little longer than four seconds to get up. I tried to be diplomatic and asked the Ewok leads if they wanted to sit this out.

"No way Kev, you have had all the fun. We're going to do this stunt ourselves." They all nodded assuring each other. Alrighty then, I walked back to my place in line on the rope.

"We're going to tie you all in," said J.R. as the stunt team made slip ties around our wrists so that even if we did let go, we would be attached to the rope. "When we pull on the rope give us resistance so it looks real. Try to stay standing."

*Try?*

As I started to get my head on, I noticed our rope was attached to a very long rope. One of the English Ewoks yelled, "I hope you have enough muscle to win this tug of war. We are pretty strong here, me and my mates!"

I heard J.R. chuckle and say, "I don't know. That's what take two is all about."

*Take two?*

We were all suited up and in our places. We went through our actions as we prepared to take down the enemy. Peter, our director, yelled, "Action!" as the imaginary walker approached. I readied myself and adjusted my grip. My feet pawed at the ground to get a good stance. I was ready. Peter yelled, "Now PULL!"

We pulled. Then we got yanked. I think we all flew. I must have been airborne for at least ten feet. Then I landed. Then I was dragged. Dirt, bugs, and muck flowed into my head and yes, into my mouth. My arm felt like it was being yanked out of the socket.

Suddenly we stopped and I heard, "Get up, get up!"

I struggled to my feet and tried to spit the garbage out of my mouth while trying to get a hold of the rope.

We heard, "PULL!"

I now knew what to expect, but I still flew. That time, though, I went with it and as I landed, I ran so I didn't fall. I ran right over one of the English Ewoks, who never was able to stand up. I now fell over him. Tony fell over me. We were a tangled mess. More dirt and twigs got into our costumes. The pulling stopped.

"Get up, get up!"

We tried to untangle ourselves. Tony had to get up before I could. I told him to grab the rope. I stood up and tried to help another Ewok up. I couldn't get a good grip on him. He just got to his feet and was about to grab the rope when we heard another, "PULL!"

Oh no! I didn't have a good grip on the rope or good footing at all. The tug came and away we went. All of us now were just being pulled into the air and then drug for, you guessed it . . . four seconds.

Mercifully we heard, "Cut."

Some of the guys just lay there. Others slowly got up. The wardrobe ladies came over and removed our heads. We spit out whatever it was that made its way into our mouths. I shook out my costume, attempting to remove any loose dirt or rocks. Production brought over some water. I swished the water around my mouth and spit out what looked like mud. I rolled my tongue across my teeth to make sure none were missing. They were all there. One more rinse of my mouth, and I chugged the bottle.

J.R. came over and told us we looked great. He asked when we would be up to doing another take. I wondered, *if we did so great, why did we need to do another take?* He realized we were not in the most chipper of moods.

Peter started buttering everyone up. "You guys were great. We just need a safety," he said.

The English Ewoks looked worse than us. They were not stunt guys. I was hoping they would say "no" to another take. I think they were about to when Warwick chimed in, "That was fun. Let's do it again. Fellas, what did you think?" Warwick nodded and said he was ready for another go.

I gave Chris and Felix a stare. They gave me a stare back. We did not want to do this stunt again but if the kids wanted to do it again? Well then, one more time on the rollercoaster. I gave a look to one of the English Ewoks, who still managed to flash his signature smile, even though he was not looking too excited.

The English Ewoks all nodded and said, "Alright gents, let's have another go." Damn kid!

"Great," I said farcically. We took a little more time to gather ourselves. If the kid could do it, the stunt guys had to do it. We got a few more rocks out of our costumes and helped each other up. We staggered back into place.

I looked over to see who was pulling us. My eyes followed the rope . . . a massive number of crewmembers stood, ready to pull at the other end. This was a tug of war we were going to lose. There must have been fifty guys! Anyone not working on the shot was pulling the rope. Teamster drivers, grips, carpenters, and anyone else—all pulling the rope. The sight of all these men pulling us reminded me of the classic tug of war scenes where one team is drastically undermanned. That was us!

As usual, the Greens Men had made everything look pretty. They had replaced all the shrubs our bodies had dug up while being drug. We were ready for take two. Now that we all knew what to expect, I mentioned to everyone to try going with the tug. "Don't try to fight it," I suggested. "Just run and stay standing."

They all agreed. We suited up. The wardrobe ladies had cleaned out our heads as well as they could. My mouth felt a random piece of dirt. That was the least of my worries. I spit it out and we all got attached to the rope and secured our footing. We were as ready as we were going to be. We all gave the thumbs up.

"Action!"

We went through our tactical actions leading up to the Ewok's overestimation of tripping the walker. We were all just a little hesitant because we knew what was about to happen. I adjusted my grip.

I heard someone yell, "Ready boys." We were as ready as we would ever be.

Peter yelled, "Pull!" and we are off to the races. I felt the gigantic tug and tried to run with it. I was doing fine until a bush—or an Ewok—tripped me up. I went down. I tried to keep my head up to avoid eating dirt. We were dragged for what seemed like an eternity. Then suddenly, we stopped and heard, "Get up, get up!"

I struggled to stand. I made it. I had no idea if anyone else did. I was ready for the next pull. Someone yelled at the guys pulling us and that got my testosterone level up. That was the wrong thing to do. I felt macho so I tried to pull back. Wrong thing, Kev. I flew through the air again and landed on my stomach. I tried to right myself while holding the rope. The guy in front of me and the guy behind me had fallen down. I tried to stand. It was no use. I went down too. We stopped again.

Discombobulated and exhausted, we tried to get up. I managed to stand. I had no more energy. I held onto the rope. I knew what was coming; I had been counting in my head. I flew again. My body was limp. I tried to hang on and keep my mouth closed, but I needed air . . . I took a big breath. Mud and muck came in with the small bit of air. I was being pulled and I was swallowing up and spitting out the entire forest. We stopped. I thanked the Lord. I felt the Force was not with me that day.

All of us Ewoks were on the ground. None of us were moving—except the kids—Warwick and his buddy. I slowly sat up. The wardrobe ladies came to our recue and removed our heads. I sat there spitting and blowing dirt out of my nose. Someone brought us water. As much as

I wanted to drink, I rinsed my mouth out a few times then swallowed the divine liquid. I poured the rest over my head.

We all just sat there and tried to joke about our stunt. The crew, who were all waiting to see if we had to do the shot again, started shouting. They tried to cheer us on for one more take. I looked to the other guys. We were lucky to get take two let alone take three.

Peter, our fearless leader, came over and gave us all a pep talk on how they needed just one more. I stayed silent. The other stunt guys stayed silent. We did not want to do another take. We were waiting for the actors to speak up. We, being the stunt guys, couldn't say "no," but the actors could. Those guys looked at each other and very slowly agreed. I dropped my head. I didn't want another take. I thought they had what they needed. We all slowly got up, grumbling about having to do another drag through the mud.

The sun had shifted a little so the techs adjusted the lighting to accommodate as we got to our places. I was so frustrated, I started yelling at the crew who were going to drag us again. It was not a nasty yell. More like a stand-up comedian. I roasted them, insulting their looks, their mother, their father, and of course their manhood. The other guys got into it, too.

The crew started yelling back. It was a smorgasbord of insults. The boys and I started getting our energy back. Even as our heads were going on, we were yelling insults back and forth. Our sour emotions got a little better. We were going to get the snot beat out of us but we were not going to let it ruin our day. "Action," was called and we, like before, didn't stand a chance. We were lifted into the air and dragged for four seconds.

When we stopped, a strange thing happened. We all found the energy to stand and fling more insults at our opponents. We shook our fists, full of machismo, when we were flung in the air again. We ate dirt for four seconds. When the tugging stopped, we struggled to our feet and yelled at the crew. Not as hardy as before—we realized we needed to save what little energy we had left.

I kept it up. The yelling seemed to give me strength. One last,

"You're so ugly," joke and I was airborne with my mates. We had lost every bit of our energy and just let the rope pull us. We had nothing more to give. Then it stopped. No more tugging at our arms. We were still, lying motionless in the forest. I could hear birds chirping. *Was I dead?* No, because I could taste the dirt in my mouth.

The wardrobe ladies came over, took our heads off, and offered us water. I struggled to muster the energy to take a sip. In the distance, I heard a strange noise . . . was it clapping?

We looked at each other as we struggled to our feet. At the other end of the rope . . . the crew was clapping, applauding. For who, we all wondered? What happened over there?

J.R. came over. He smiled and pointed at the crew. "They're applauding you," he said. The forest echoed as the crew clapped and yelled our praises. I couldn't help but smile.

We all broke out into a great big laugh. We were so tired but this was the cherry on what was a very tough start of a day. I may have had a tear well up. Maybe it was something in my eye. There was a lot of dust and dirt being flung around. We were all very touched. Warwick went out and took a bow. That brought the house down.

# Chapter Thirty-One
# Healthy Competition

I HAD BROUGHT WITH me two Stuntman's Association belt buckles from home. I was going to use them to trade. I had made a T-shirt trade with one of the English Ewoks when I first arrived. He gave me one from London with a special effects company logo and I gave him a Warner Brothers Studio shirt from California. When I got back to my room, I realized that two people deserved the buckles more than I needed them for a good trade.

During lunch, I stood up and made an announcement. I began describing our adventure in trying to trip the walker. I didn't need to embellish on how the entire crew had a grand time with our tug-of-war scene. I thanked the crew for the ovation on behalf of the guys. I spoke about how tough it was and how two guys never complained, our two youngest Ewoks, Warwick and his buddy. "Boys, come over here and receive your honorary Stuntman's belt buckle."

The whole place stood up and gave them a standing ovation. The look on their faces was better than any trade I could have ever made. Their smiles are forever embedded in my heart. I wonder if they still have those belt buckles. The buckles were bigger than them.

We, the stunt Ewoks, were dog-tired and starving. Lunch was good and the chatter from the crew was great. It was funny . . . yelling insults at each other actually brought us all closer. During lunch we had some more good-natured ribbing. I made sure I didn't eat too much. I had a whole afternoon of running ahead of me.

I think the English actors were sent back to the motel. I didn't see them for the rest of the day. We stunt guys had set up our afternoon shots before lunch, so we knew what we were in for. We were to run through the bushes while explosions went off. We would walk a route that J.R. had mapped out. He had pointed at a spot where a mortar was and said, "Boom. The last guy in the line dies." Then we'd continue walking. J.R. pointed at another spot and said, "Boom, no one dies, everyone keeps running, shot ends."

Shooting scenes after lunch was always a little harder. Our under-fur padding never quite dried out. Our feet and gloves were always just a bit damp, much like the feeling of putting on a wet bathing suit. It was weird because in one sense I liked it because it kept me cool for a bit. In the other, I was swimming in my own sweat. At least it was *my* sweat, I reasoned.

As I started getting dressed, I felt little pieces of sticks and twigs. Wardrobe had tried to get the stuff out of the costume as much as possible, but hadn't managed to get it all. I had to live with it. Wardrobe told me it would be better the next day. But for now, I had to run and bear it with the little stick poking me in the back of my buttocks. The afternoon would be fun.

We lined up to do our first rehearsal run after lunch. I nominated myself to be last. Michael and Chris wanted to lead the charge. Felix and Tony were taken over to another area of the forest to do another stunt set-up. Ewok extras were put in line with us. They would be running by the mortars. They were told that they would not be close to them as they exploded. We all told Butch not to yodel. He didn't listen.

As tired as Michael, Chris, and I were, we could not complain because we were now incorporated with the extras. The stunt guys would do every take. The extras would be folded in and out of the different takes to give a sense of change in doing the same scene. We would change our Ewok running order to make the same camera setup look like different locations. The extras were a little nervous as we walked our route. Their eyes went wide when they realized how close they would be to the mortars. J.R. asked if they were nervous to speak up now and say if they didn't want to do the scene. They all agreed to do it.

Debbie was one of the hardest workers and she really wanted to make the stunt team. She was a firecracker. She was giving Chris and Michael a hard time about who was faster. That was not the day any of us wanted to be tested by the extra team. They were all in shape and wanted to show J.R. that they could do their job. They didn't care that we had already done a day's work during the morning. Even after lunch I was spitting small bits of dirt out of my mouth. The extras didn't care. I wouldn't have either. I wanted to show J.R. what I could do.

We suited up and "Action," was called. We all started and *BOOM* went the mortar. I felt the power of the blast against my back. I didn't have to act very hard to make believe I was blown off my feet. The explosion helped me just fine.

I heard, "Cut!" and started to get up. The wardrobe ladies removed my head and I heard Debbie boasting that she was faster than Michael and Chris. She probably was. We were beat up already and not in the mood to be challenged. But we *were* challenged the rest of the day. Even Butch, when he wasn't yodeling, was running as fast as he could.

I looked at Chris and Michael. We had to praise them for their athleticism and suck up their ribbing. They would rest after a take and then come in fresh.

I was trying to keep up with them on this one take. I tripped on a bush and went down. I turned my fall into a front somersault and popped right back up and kept running! That was fresh competition and J.R. loved it. He wanted to see how his stuntmen would react when challenged on one of the hardest days on the job. We were too busy worrying about being shown up by the speed of the extra performers that we forgot about how tired we were. They beat us a few times and they let us know it. We just had to smile and take it. It came with the job. Before lunch we received a standing ovation from the crew. After lunch we were beaten down by the extras. That was life on Endor.

# Chapter Thirty-Two
## Making Amends

DEBBIE NEEDED TO make amends. I wasn't in the scene but I heard about it from Felix.

Two stormtroopers were shooting at Han Solo and Chewbacca. The Ewoks were to attack and overpower them. Everyone went through the rehearsals and it was time to put one on film. We suited up and, "Action," was called. The stormtroopers started shooting. The Ewoks attacked and took them down. As the Ewoks used their weapons to stage hit the stormtroopers, Debbie accidentally clocked Felix in the head. Debbie had really gotten into character and Felix was in the way of her club. Felix was knocked down but not hurt.

After they cut, Debbie ran away, feeling embarrassed. Felix followed her and found her hiding behind a tree almost crying. He asked her if he looked like a stormtrooper. I would have said yes, but she said, "No."

He continued with fatherly advice because he was quite a bit older than her and had a few more years of experience under his belt. He looked at her and said, "We're on the same team. If we make a mistake, accept it, apologize and move on. Don't run away and hide like it didn't happen. I was clocked many times by other Ewok actors but they didn't run away. We made amends right away."

I think Felix wanted to make sure that she knew that when mistakes happen, we needed to take responsibility for our actions.

Debbie was part of one of the most famous and favorite scenes. Many times, for an actor, whether featured or in the background, one doesn't know how the scene will play for an audience. There were so many scenes that all of us were a part of; some made it into the movie, some hit the cutting room floor. That's just how it goes.

Debbie did a scene where two Ewoks run and one gets hit by a mortar and dies. She doesn't leave the side of her fallen friend. The other Ewok's part was easy—he had to run and fall down when the mortar went off, playing dead. Debbie's was harder. With the head on we could not show eye or facial movements. We all used body language, head nodding or shaking, hand gestures . . . whatever we could think to do. We had to bring the emotion from our gut and produce it through our big heavy costume. It was tough. It could be too big and over the top, making it unbelievable or it could be too small and the audience wouldn't see any reaction at all.

Debbie had to run, fall, get up, try and help the Ewok, and then realize he was dead. She slumped in sorrow, without showing any facial expressions. She did a great job. Her acting came through and the audience felt her emotions that made us all weep. It was a bravo moment for the two of them and I was really happy for her. Moments like those made us proud of our Ewok team. A win for one was a win for all.

# Chapter Thirty-Three
## San Francisco or Bust

ONE DAY, I was told I would be doing a scene with Chewbacca, helping him hijack an Imperial walker. My stunt buddy and I stripped off our costumes and put on our harnesses. When it was time for the stunt, Chewy and the two of us stunt Ewoks would swing in together. We were excited.

I noticed the special effects guys and J.R. talking and pointing. The wardrobe ladies came over and took our costumes over to the prop guys and they began stuffing our costumes to make it look like we were inside. J.R. came over and broke the news: we would not be doing the stunt. There would be too much weight on the rope with all three of us swinging. We were replaced by stuffed costumes! How humiliating.

The prop guys attached the two Ewoks to Chewbacca's legs and he swung on top of the walker. The stuffing made me look great; I had to admit, with a tad of jealousy.

The crew had attached a replica walker to a forklift whose blades were up, about twelve-feet high. As we performed the rest of the scene, the forklift functioned as if it was walking on legs—starting and stopping in herky jerky movements. We got back into our costumes and climbed on the walker. It was crazy and really unstable on top of our makeshift walker. The hatch opened and Chewie grabbed the driver and threw him out. We jumped down into the walker and Chewie joined us.

Production told us that we would continue the scene another day, probably at ILM, George Lucas's secret studios. Oh, boy!

At lunch my stunt buddy and I tried to keep the fact that we would be going to San Francisco to work at ILM a secret. The usual lunch talk was going on. The chicken was dry. What was the fish, *really*? The food in San Francisco would be a welcome change. Not that the food on set was bad. It just would be a lot different.

I wanted to tell our secret so bad. Tony sat down with us and started talking about how Dave and Bill told him he was going to San Francisco. They were making the travel arrangements. I looked over at my other buddy. He looked at me. *What had happened?* We got up to talk with Dave and Bill.

We found them outside the commissary tent and asked why we weren't going. They told us we were too valuable to leave the forest. We had another big week of stunts coming up. Oh, well. No San Francisco for me. I had been getting all excited over nothing.

I went back to finish my lunch and talked with Felix. He also thought he was going to San Francisco. He told me about a hang-gliding stunt he had just done. It was a rig attached to a jeep, about ten feet in the air. The camera's point of view made it look like he was flying. The driver pretended to fly as he drove and Felix mimicked his movements. If the driver turned right, Felix would bank like he was turning right, in the air. Felix was told they'd have to do some blue screen work at ILM, so he was disappointed to hear he wasn't going as well.

Regardless, we had to keep our spirits up… there was still plenty of fun ahead for us in the forest.

# Chapter Thirty-Four
# Walking a Fine Line

AFTER LUNCH, I got dressed and a bunch of us took a couple of jeeps to a new location. Production wanted us to run across a huge fallen tree and shoot our bow and arrows. As it often happened, it sounded much simpler than it was.

The tree was a giant redwood and the diameter was about the size of a car. On its side it was literally ten feet high, so we needed a ladder to climb to the top. All the padding made climbing the ladder a chore in itself. Once we made it, we would run across the tree's rough and uneven bark in a single file, shoot our arrows, and run away. If we ran off course or tripped, we would fall to the ground below - no crash pads for us. I wanted to lead the charge because that way, there wasn't anyone in front to trip me up, but Chris was chosen and I was stuck in the middle.

We practiced a few times with our heads off and just couldn't get the spacing right. Some were running too fast and some were too slow. Wendy, the choreographer, changed the lineup and I got to lead because I kept a better pace. Chris was too fast. Same logistics as before, but our sight would be impaired with our heads. We would count our steps to reach our marks and had to keep straight and true to stay on the tree. Once we were ready, we suited up and the prop guys gave us our weapons.

The whole thing was quite tricky. Even after we had run across the log, we couldn't see to climb down the ladder to get out of the camera's view. It was hard to feel the arrow through the thickness of the gloves. Chris, who was now behind me, started razzing me about leading everyone off the log. Someone else chimed in and we were up there yakking at each other when "Action," was called.

I took off. I had to count six steps. That was my mark. I stopped. I raised my bow and fired then, turned around and ran. I heard Chris right behind me. I counted to eight and stopped. Chris stopped behind me but someone crashed into him and knocked us both down. We are still on the tree but not on our feet. We were on our bellies, hanging on to the tree wondering what just happened.

Someone had forgotten to count steps and came in like a bowling ball, knocking us all down like pins. Our shock turned into a good chuckle. No one got hurt and no one claimed responsibility. Production helped us up and the wardrobe gals took off our heads. As we went back to our start marks, wardrobe wiped out the sweat and cleared the fog off our lenses. Prop reloaded our arrows and we moved on to take two.

We lined up, ready for action, and someone dropped an arrow. The ladder came out and lickity split, the arrow was given back to the Ewok that had dropped it. "Action!"

We ran, I counted my steps, got to the number six, stopped and shot. Then I ran for my exit. We all made it safe to the other side of the log. Production asked if we could do another without removing our heads. It became routine, take after take. There was a little grumbling but we all agreed.

I can't emphasize enough how poor our eyesight was with our heads on. We were basically blind. We had to use our other senses. I felt the curve of the tree and told the others to run on top of the arch. It was hard because once I deviated from the curve of the tree, it would lead me off course and I'd fall. We lined up. No chatting. No joking around. Sweat was dripping into my eyes. I blinked hard, trying to relieve the stinging.

"Action," was called and we ran again. I felt the curve and ran onto it, hoping the others did, too. I stopped and fired my arrow, and then ran for the exit. We all felt it was a good take and thankfully, production did, too. But . . . we still did the scene another five times!

We were tired, but with the constant repetition of the scene, we had become very comfortable. We were warriors of the forest and running on logs was simply what we did. Finally, it was time to move on. Check the gate!

# Chapter Thirty-Five
# Falling Rock

FOR THE NEXT couple of days, we did a lot of running scenes and I understood why I was kept in the forest instead of going to San Francisco. We were constantly running in different set ups and different scenes with explosions, on fallen trees and over bushes. Many of the Ewok extras were only good for a few takes because the outfits were so hot, heavy, and cumbersome. Then a fresh batch of extras would join us. They were like chocolate chip cookies, fresh out of the oven and ready to be eaten. It kind of was that way. Their energy was eaten up, fast and hot. We would all do a lot more running until they got tired. By that time, the guys and I were bushed. We were hot, wet, and sticky. Production would then realize how it was affecting us and give us a little bit less strenuous work.

When it was time to move on, a bunch of us jumped in a couple of jeeps and took off to another part of the forest. We looked like GI's hanging all over the jeep. It was made for four people, but I believe there were about eight of us. I know we are half the size of average size people, but I'm sure it was a sight to be seen. As we rambled through the forest, we hung on to each other so we didn't fall out.

I liked riding in the jeep and was always ready for a new adventure. I never knew what was next, because I knew not to ask J.R. I wondered if secretly he didn't really know, but didn't want to let on that he didn't know. Everyone was flying by the seat of their pants and I was flying in the jeep hanging onto my pants.

We came up to the new set: a bridge. In the scene we would throw rocks at the stormtroopers below. The stunt team was down in a valley under the bridge. They were good heartedly yelling at us to get dressed and do the scene. I didn't have any idea how long they had been waiting for us.

We all got out of the jeeps, and in a single file line, went out and inspected the bridge. It was less than three feet wide, and made of rickety wood. The slats were not uniform and there were many spaces between them. No ropes or railings were present on either side of the bridge—it really did look like we, the Ewoks, had made it. The valley floor was about twenty to thirty feet below. If we fell, we might be killed. But that was all part of the job, or at least that's what J.R. had me believe. We could very easily put our foot right through the slats. But of course, we had to put those negative thoughts out of our minds.

We were again mixed in with the extra Ewoks. As we walked onto the bridge, we realized it wasn't level. We had trouble keeping our balance. One of the Ewoks stumbled too close to the edge and began going down face first. Thankfully, a big hand grabbed the back of his neck like a mama cat grabbing her kitten to safety. He was back upright on his feet, but out of breath. We continued on.

There were stacks of Styrofoam rocks all evenly spaced on the bridge. We were to stand there and throw our rocks at the storm-troopers below. We all looked at each other with a devilish grin because we couldn't wait . . . we already had lots of practice throwing rocks at the plastic porta-potty hut.

When it was time to get off the bridge and get dressed, half the wardrobe ladies headed into the valley to help the stunt stormtroopers get ready. That took a little time. The crew set up to find their shots. We had not even had a rehearsal, but we were okay with that. We just wanted to do the shot and get off the bridge without falling.

The stunt Ewoks would be out in the middle of the bridge. We would have the more treacherous walk to our places and back. I got dressed and started my slow but steady walk toward the middle, between Michael and Chris. We gingerly scooted by the many piles of rocks so as to not upset them.

I arrived at my spot, and with my head, went over the logistics of where the edge of the bridge was. I inched my toe over to the side until I felt air. Woops, that was far enough. My rock pile was to my right. I tried to pick up a rock. They were so light. Just like everything else, they were hard to grip with the gloves. Now, I had to remember they were supposed to be heavy. Okay, I was ready. "Action!"

I remembered my mime skills and gave weight to the Styrofoam boulders. I picked them up and heaved them at my adversaries down below. I threw a little too hard and almost lost my balance. I tried to look over to see who I was throwing at, but I could only see shadows. I picked up another and continue until my rock pile was gone. Since they didn't cut, I jumped up and down and shook my fist at the storm-troopers. With nothing to do, I had to improvise to keep the scene going. Finally, I heard, "Cut!"

Production was yelling about something. All I knew was we are going to do it again. We slowly made the trek across the bridge to where the wardrobe ladies were. They took off our heads. I noticed that production wasn't yelling. They were laughing. Apparently when we were throwing the rocks, the wind took them. The stunt stormtroopers tried to get hit by these snowflake boulders. Being on a steep hillside and looking up, these guys were falling all over the place, trying to look like they were receiving massive blows to the head by these feather-light rocks!

I was told that the view out of the stormtroopers head was much like the view from underwater looking out—shadows, nothing more. They were having a heck of a time just trying to keep their balance. The steep incline was close to a 45-degree angle. That was hard enough just to stand on, let alone in a cumbersome costume looking up. I watched them trying to get back to their start marks and they were still falling all over the place. It was hard not to laugh—the shoe was on the other foot. Usually the crew was laughing at us Ewoks. Now we enjoyed the chuckle. It really was a family unit, all with the same goal of making magic in the most magical movie.

We did a few more takes from those same camera angles. The stunt guys were still having a heck of a time down in the valley. Production moved the camera angle so that they could get some close-ups on some of the rocks that hit the stormtroopers. The prop guys threw the rocks at them from just out of view of the camera. At least they were falling at the right time.

Production then changed the shot to show a different point of view, down in the valley. The crew's laughter turned to grumbling. They now had to haul all the equipment down into the valley. They started slipping and sliding with all their gear. I was so glad that we did not have to be in that dang valley of discord at that time. They set the shot up. It was on us Ewoks on the bridge. We did it a few times. I did my best mime of heavy rocks as did the other Ewoks.

"Cut, print, check the gate!" We got out of there.

Now came the hard part. The crew had to get all the equipment they brought down, back up. The team worked together and their precision was amazing. I was getting out of my costume as ropes came down and the crew was directing the excavation of the equipment back up. In a way it was easier than them trying to get down and set up. The sun was setting and production called it a day. Everyone was glad to be done with the dang valley.

# Chapter Thirty-Six
## In Reverse

ON THE RIDE home, I noticed Daniel Frishman, one of the Ewok extras, was not on the bus. Daniel was a Shakespearian actor who I had worked with in the Michael Dunn Theater. Someone mentioned that he wasn't feeling well. Part of me was amazed that more people didn't call in sick, but I knew the reason. There were no "sick days." If you didn't come in to work, you didn't get paid.

Daniel had driven up in his own truck, but when we arrived back at the motel that day, it was gone. He returned a few days later and made no mention of where he had been. I guess it really was none of our business. Daniel was quiet and tough. The joke on set was that he ate his lunch in his Ewok costume. He never complained. He was the first one in, and the last one out. I found out where he went a few months later—on an audition for a lead in a feature film, *Lone Wolf McQuade*. He landed the part as the main bad guy in the only film featuring Chuck Norris and David Carradine. That was a big gamble leaving for a few days, but it paid off. I was very happy for him.

The next day, I had to work several different scenes swinging on a rope. J.R. was not there, so the stunt team coordinated the scenes with me. The first one I was to do was really strange. I got in my harness, pulled on my stunt quilt, and put my Ewok fur over it. I had a little hole in the stomach area of my costume where a carabineer stuck out. It was a different hole than the one used when I swung across the valley.

The wardrobe ladies sewed it up and gave me a new head so that I appeared to be someone else. I headed over to where my scene was to take place.

The camera was placed high on the scaffolding, pointing down. The special effects guys were rigging my rope with a quick release hook called a Pelican hook. As I got attached to the rope, I was also attached to a wire that brought me up so that I would be parallel to the ground. The wardrobe ladies suited me up. I made sure that I was safely attached. As we were going through all these check points, my stunt coordinators asked if I knew what I was doing. I shook my head. Nope.

They explained that I was grabbing a vine, fall off the snorkel lift, and swing on it. The plan was to film me falling backwards. In postproduction they would reverse the film to make it look like I was swinging up to a tree. I was told to keep my legs up and as I fell, to slowly bring my legs back. I thought about those old flipbooks with the pictures of a bird landing. I then thought about how when I was a kid, I liked to flip it the opposite way. That was my action. I told them I was ready and the special effects guys hauled me up.

As I was pulled up, I could feel the Earth's gravity pulling me away from the rope. I had to wrap my legs around the rope to stay in position, so that I was parallel to the ground. The camera operator wanted to see what I looked like as I did my action. I unhooked my legs and struggled to show him. My stomach muscles ached from working so hard to keep my legs up. My arms were burning from keeping me still. They told me they had it and to relax. Relax? I struggled to wrap my legs back around the rope. I wondered when we are going to shoot. Both the cumbersome costume and gravity were really tiring me out.

"Roll cameras. Action!"

All of a sudden, I was falling. My heart was pounding. The feeling of falling was so overwhelming that I forget to unwrap my legs around the rope. I swung down and didn't even remember to do the whole leg action. I was so embarrassed.

The wardrobe ladies took my head off. The guys were all chuckling at me. "Felt kind of weird, eh, Kev? Next time don't look so surprised."

It felt like being on a tree branch that suddenly snapped. That was the Pelican hook. A trip wire was attached so it could be released. I didn't realize that the fall would be that immediate. I would be ready the next time.

My head went back on and the crew pulled me up to my start mark. I hung on like I did before. As I waited, I heard the camera people say they were glad I flubbed it. Now they knew the focus marks. We would have had to do it again anyway because I would have been out of focus. I felt a little better. It wasn't just me.

The orders were yelled and the camera started rolling. They asked if I was ready. I nodded and got my legs into landing mode, in front of me. My stomach muscles tightened as I heard, "Action."

I started my fall and began to bring my legs back. It still felt weird but it did seem better than the previous take, now that I knew what to expect. Production was much happier with my performance, too, but I did it five more times. I was so curious to see what I was jumping off of once it was on the big screen. I would soon have a clue.

Tony and two of the female Ewok extras made it back from San Francisco and filled us in on their adventure. Actually, they said they had been in San Rafael, about twenty minutes north of San Francisco. They talked of room service and cloth napkins. We were in awe. The dampness of the forest, the smell of mud, and the motel life was getting old. Don't get me wrong, I loved the woods. It was just a change that we all wanted for even a short while.

They knew how we felt and saw how we hung to their every word. They started talking about how they had dinner with George Lucas at his home, drinking cognac by the fireplace. Then went with it for a little while before busting up. They couldn't keep the charade up any longer. I think we might have even believed them if they had played it down at least a little bit. It was fun giving each other a hard time as if I was back home with my brothers and sisters.

Embellishments aside, they *did* tell us all about the things they filmed there at the mysterious ILM studios. We huddled close, eager, and yes, a little jealous, as we took in every detail.

# Chapter Thirty-Seven
## ILM Secrets

ILM, GEORGE LUCAS's private studio, stands for Industrial Light and Magic. It is known for cutting edge special effects. Tony told us he had done many different scenes with stunts and a green screen. He told us more about the speeder bikes and explained the stormtroopers chased us through the forest. Production had tried to explain it to us but Tony's explanation really opened up our eyes.

Kenny Baker's Ewok steals the speeder bike. Tony was stunt doubling for Kenny. Production put the speeder bike on a cable and attached it to the ceiling. Then they pointed it straight up and attached Tony's hands to the handlebars so he couldn't let go. The camera was placed on its side next to him on a rig. This rig allowed the camera to follow Tony up to the ceiling. As Tony, on the speeder bike, traveled to the ceiling, the camera on the rig followed. The effect would make it look like Tony was travelling so fast he was flying.

I asked how he got off the speeder bike and he told of reaching up for a rope. Now I realized what that stunt was that I had just done. I was the Ewok swinging off the speeder bike. The stunt guys didn't always know why we were doing what we did, but the filmmakers knew what they were doing. Thank goodness someone did!

The female Ewok extras chimed in about how their characters fought in the cockpit of the Imperial walker. I asked if they got bumped up to a stunt performer. They said they got a little stunt bump, but not a contract like Tony and the other stunt guys. I felt bad and hoped they would all be compensated for their stunt work.

I felt very lucky that I had the stunt contract. During my first movie, I didn't have a stunt contract, and it made it feel like production took advantage of me. If these women felt this way, they didn't show it. They were always very professional.

All of the ladies playing Ewoks, were tough. They rode that bus back and forth to work and got dirty, hot, and sweaty wearing the Ewok costume. Just wearing the costume was hard enough but they were running, jumping, and falling down all day. Day after day they were giving me a run for my money, trying to outdo me.

I didn't want to lose to them. Those lady Ewoks were giving me a good dose of kidding, saying they were just as fast. They may have been. I was not going to let them know that. I was nervous as heck thinking I would fall down and they would chide me. They were tough and they knew I knew it.

# Chapter Thirty-Eight
## Up for the Challenge

THE ILM ADVENTURES were retold over the bus ride to work. We were feeling a bit cooped up and were happy to hear stories from the outside. When we arrived at the location, J.R. came up to all the stunt guys and told us to dress in the pajamas and meet him by the workout area.

We ate light and headed over to find a mini-tamp set up along with a couple of twelve-inch-thick crash pads. A mini-tramp is a three-foot-wide trampoline set at an angle about a foot off the ground.

"I need to see who can fly the farthest off a mini-tramp," J.R. said.

This would be the first stunt of the day. I was glad I ate light. I used to perform on the mini-tramp in high school and also had done a mini-tramp stunt on a film a few years earlier. I felt confident.

We all lined up to give it a go. We needed to run about fifteen steps to get up to speed. Then we'd jump and fly into the air at least ten feet. I was last in line. The guys were jumping and landing on their feet on the pad like they were jumping off a couch or a running broad jump. J.R. was shaking his head. I saw him mutter to himself that we needed distance. All of a sudden one of the guys did a trick called a brany. It is a flip with a half twist. That looked pretty cool. J.R. liked that but he stressed more distance.

When it was my turn, I decided to do something different. If I did it wrong, I could break my neck. It was a flying dive roll. I ran and hit the mini-tramp with both feet at the same time. I flew like I had just dived off a diving board. Right before I landed, I tucked my head into my chest and rolled out.

I looked at J.R. He was smiling. "That's what I want. Who else can do that?"

Everyone now asked me how I did the trick. To me, I had been doing it for as long as I could remember. It was probably the thing that gave my mother her first grey hair. I explained it and was about to do it again when J.R. made a mark and told us we must travel at least ten feet in the air. I took my run and flew just short of the mark. Chris and Michael took their turns and did well. Felix and Tony decided the stunt wasn't for them and bowed out. The other guy did his brany again. That was a neat trick but he wasn't getting the distance.

To do a dive roll is a mind-blowing experience. Chris and Michael were trying to get the distance. Michael landed wrong and took himself out of the competition. My next try I really jumped hard onto the mini-tramp. As I did, I knew I flew farther than before. I looked up. J.R. was standing with the mark. I was just short. He nodded though—he knew I was getting better. Chris could not increase his distance and the continuous brany trick wasn't doing anything for J.R. If I could get the distance, the stunt was mine. I went back and was ready to jump.

J.R. yelled, "We are changing it up!"

The stunt team brought over a four-foot platform. I was now to jump from the platform to the mini-tramp to the pad. That was different. I had timed the jump with the speed of my run. Now the weight of my jump from the platform sent me flying. I was able to fly the desired distance, ten feet. The other guys tried the platform jump and couldn't get far enough.

J.R. told me to get dressed. All this time only J.R. knew what the stunt was. I was not about to ask him. Do my job and don't ask questions. I did the practice stunt in my costume without my head on one time. Everything went fine. We loaded into the jeep.

The ride was only about five minutes. We came up to the set: a couple of logs that had fallen in a forty-five-degree angle. The prop and special effects crew were busy doing their finishing touches. I looked over the set pieces trying to figure out what I was going to do. Where were we hiding the mini-tramp? We would have to hide it. Ewoks didn't have mini-tramps, or did they?

I headed over and saw the special effects guys finishing up a mortar. I realized what I was about to do when J.R. came over and explained the shot. He pointed to the fatter log that was not much taller - more like ten feet high. He then pointed his finger and my eyes followed to show my route. We would place the mini-tramp at the base of the log. I would bounce off that and over the other fallen log onto the crash pad ten feet away. As we set up the mini-tramp I thought, *This was not quite what we had been rehearsing.* There was a mortar right behind the mini-tramp.

I climbed up to the top of the fallen log with J.R. and my wardrobe lady following behind. Those wardrobe ladies are tough, too. They kicked butt. I looked down at the mini-tramp. It looked a lot further down than ten feet. The pad looked a lot further away, too. Special effects would execute the explosion after my jump. They hoped to time it with the upward motion from the mini-tramp. Wow, it seemed complicated. I was *really* glad I had a light breakfast. Everyone was ready and I finished getting dressed. They were going to shoot the rehearsal. It was lightning in a bottle.

Since I couldn't see the mini-tramp once my head was on, I asked my wardrobe lady to dress me at my launch spot. I'd be jumping blind. Again, I had to stay calm. All I had to do was faithfully step out and hit the mini-tramp. I hoped.

Cameras started rolling and production yelled, "Any time, Kev." I jumped, trying not to think about missing the mini-tramp . . . I hit it perfectly. I heard the blast of the mortar and felt the heat from it as I started my flight. As I was flying, I hoped I was able to clear the other log. I tucked my head to my chest instinctively and rolled on to the mat, safe.

Production yelled, "Cut," and I heard the crew clapping with excitement. Wardrobe removed my head and I saw smiles all around.

I was not hurt. It was actually really fun, but I hoped we had the shot. We were probably going to have to do another one for safety. The stunt guys pulled me up and gave me a good-hearted slap on the back. Production gave the special effects team a thumbs up. They checked the gate. It was good. Production jokingly yelled, "We're on the wrong set. Let's get out of here." We did the shot in one take. Yes! It was a satisfying relief.

Kudos tend to last only so long, and in a flash, it was time to move to the next shot. I jumped in a jeep and headed to another part of the forest. We pulled up in time for me to see the stunt Ewoks working with bolas. A bola is a rope with weighted balls attached to the ends. The balls are about the size of baseball. South American cowhands, gauchos, designed them to entangle a cow's legs. The Ewoks would be hunting stormtroopers, not cows. We stunt guys were learning something new every day. The English Ewoks had joined in, too.

I got out. I realized these guys had been practicing for a while. I was supposed to swing the bola over my head, like a cowboy with a lasso. It was harder than it looked, especially because we couldn't wear our stunt quilt for the shot. The thick padding made everything more difficult. Chris was picking it up better than the rest of us. Everybody was trying to throw it at the target—an old tree stump. I was having a heck of a time trying to learn how to throw the dang thing and didn't think I'd be doing that stunt.

J.R. asked for the three best, which did not include me. Chris, Michael, and one other guy went off to do their shot. I stayed with the English blokes. Tony and Felix jumped into a jeep to do another shot.

One of the English guys was actually pretty good at it and we all continued to practice throwing our bolas. We would have a good shot. Sometimes it flew where we didn't want it to go. As he tried to throw it, Warwick somehow wrapped it around his head. He fell down and we all went to see if he was all right. He was on the ground, laughing. So we all started laughing. We were using stunt props so they didn't actually hurt. I told Warwick to show Peter his 'stunt'. He trotted off to go show him, and Peter loved it. Warwick got his own shot. Warwick again stole the scene with his antics.

At lunch, all we could talk about was the bola scenes. The guys did a few different scenes with them. The extra Ewoks filled in the background. It showed that we were a team and everyone was contributing. It was good healthy chatter.

# Chapter Thirty-Nine
# Out on A Limb

WARDROBE CAME UP to me as I was dressing after lunch with a different head. Production had told them I was being seen too much and had to become someone different. They actually brought a few over for me to try on. None of them had any noticeable markings. They were all just different shades of brown. Production sat down with me and told me we are going to do a bunch of tree shots. I looked at them with a puzzled look. We needed to film Ewoks in the trees blowing horns, waving, and chopping ropes. I was ready. Tony would join me in the adventure.

We both hopped in a jeep and were driven to a location that I had not been to before. The camera crane was there. That was a piece of machinery that held a camera and two people. With that device, the camera department would be able to capture the scene from the right angle. There would use a cherry picker to get us up into the tree. I was glad I wasn't going to have to climb. That would have taken forever. They pointed at the branch where we would be sitting and Tony's eyes grew wide. The branch was about forty feet off the ground. Tony, though a stuntman, was not a fan of heights.

I got dressed except for my head and climbed into the bucket of the cherry picker with my trusty wardrobe gal, stunt guy, and the cherry picker operator. Up we went.

I looked out on another gorgeous valley full of redwood trees as far as the eye could see. We stopped at the chosen tree branch. Yup. We were definitely high.

The camera crew had lined up the shot on this particular branch for my scene. They were across the way on a camera crane. My wardrobe lady put my head on and I maneuvered out to try and sit on the branch. Because of the cumbersome costume, even attempting to sit on a branch was difficult. Reaching out with my hands, I grabbed the branch and pulled myself up out of the bucket, so I was lying across it. I needed to sit up and turn around, which was a little nerve-wracking. Why? I was forty feet up above the forest floor and I couldn't see because . . . Ewok eyesight.

I brought my right arm under my body to try to lift myself up and carefully turn around. Everyone in the bucket was trying to help me. As I turned, I felt like I was falling off the branch. I couldn't get my butt in position to sit on the branch. The operator in the bucket tried to help me, but it was tough. I had to start over. I climbed back into the bucket.

Everyone's eyes shifted from the tree branch to me, over and over again. We were all trying to figure out how to get me to sit on it. Finally, I realized I'd have to step out on the branch, turn around, and sit down. That would be easiest. I couldn't wear the stunt gloves or feet because it would show to camera. The real costume gloves and feet had no grip.

I told the operator to lift the bucket just a little higher. I climbed out beside the tree trunk and used it to help me balance. Then I climbed out on the branch, stood up, and continued to use the tree to stabilize myself as I turned around. It was harder than it sounded because of the costume and head, but I was able to make it work. I used my feet to find an even place to sit, trying to avoid any sharp wood protruding out of the branch. Been there done that.

Once I lowered myself and sat, the camera operator and I adjusted to find the right frame. I was handed a horn to blow. All that just so I could blow a horn? I did a couple of takes and we were done. Wow. Now, I had to get *off* the branch.

I tossed the horn back to the guys in the cherry picker. I placed my foot on the branch and the bark ripped away on the tree! I lost my balance and tightened my grip, hanging onto the tree. I was a tree hugger, literally. I slowly placed my foot on the branch and raised myself up. Then I started to do the same turn around dance while hanging onto the tree.

My stunt buddy said, "Just jump in the cherry picker bucket."

I thought that over for a second. I was forty feet up in the air and I couldn't see. I'd be jumping blind. *Why not?* I thought. I gave him the thumbs up and he counted to three.

I jumped. I flew. My stunt buddy kind of caught me and we rolled onto the floor of the cherry picker. Safe. Sheesh. It had happened before and would happen again—the set-up of the shot was a bigger stunt than the stunt itself.

I took my head off and looked down at Tony, standing on the ground below, nervously watching. It sure hadn't sounded this hard when they had explained it. We lowered down in the bucket and Tony's eyes grew bigger as we got closer. I got out and told him how much fun it was. He was not buying what I was selling.

My stunt buddy got an idea and explained to Tony that they would lift him out and place him on the tree. That way it would be easier for him to get on the tree branch. He started to think about it and with some coaching he agreed. I got out of the cherry picker and Tony got in. Up they went.

I struggled to get out of my costume as one of the crew came by and unzipped the back. I pulled my sweaty arms out of my costume and welcomed the cool breeze across my drenched baby blue pajamas. I looked up to see Tony getting ready to be placed on the branch. They had positioned the cherry picker next to a different branch. Tony was a little hesitant and I could tell he was worried. My stunt buddy was trying his best to convince Tony that everything would be okay and he reluctantly agreed.

Wardrobe put on Tony's Ewok head and he hopped into the cherry picker with our stunt buddy. The operator lifted him out of the bucket, placing him on the tree. That was a lot easier than how I climbed out on the branch.

Tony was hanging onto the tree. I felt for him because it was a weird feeling. He probably couldn't see. The mouth opening of the head was around his nose. He was forty feet in the air and they were trying to hand him a prop. Not a normal day at the office. Well, I guess it was a normal day in *this* office.

The camera crane adjusted their shot. Props held off on giving him the horn. They told him just to wave and had him do a few takes. They said they needed to adjust their shot to make it look like a different tree. Tony was not happy about having to stay on the branch, but he did realize that it would be easier for him. He wouldn't have to climb down then climb back up again for the same shot. Production knew they would save time by doing that. An experienced camera crew can save time by knowing when to combine shots. Once the camera's shot was adjusted, it looked like an entirely different tree in another part of the forest.

Props managed to give Tony an Ewok horn to pretend to blow and they did a few takes then voila . . . Tony was done.

The crew helped him out of the tree. As he came down, there was not a shred of anxiety in his voice. The old Tony was back, cracking jokes and giving me a hard time about how much trouble *I had* on the branch. We looked at each other and just started cracking up. We both knew how terrified he had been up there and now that we were back on the ground, all we could do was laugh about it.

# Chapter Forty
## Third Times a Charm

ONY JUMPED IN a jeep and headed to another part of the forest while I stayed behind with the tree crew. We had a little down time, so the wardrobe ladies helped me get out of my costume.

We waited for props to rig some ropes. The crew had to get the rope from the prop truck and place it where the camera crew wanted to compose the shot. They were dressing the scene, which means they strung the rope in the tree so that it looked like the Ewoks had strategically placed it there.

I had enough time for a break. Wardrobe had thrown a blanket out on a grassy patch for me to lay my sweaty costume on so that it could dry in the sun. I lay down next to it. I looked up at the big beautiful trees and took it in. That had been my office for the past couple of weeks. Sometimes I just didn't appreciate my surroundings. Right at that moment, I did. I closed my eyes for a bit, just listening to birds chirping, the wind blowing, the trees swaying, and the crew cursing. Heaven.

I must have dozed off because my stunt buddy slapped my feet and I jumped to attention. He just smiled at me with one of those grins that said, "Gotcha!" My heart was racing, the crew was still working and I was staring at funny boy. I picked up a cup of water and was about to throw it at him when production yelled for me to get dressed.

Laughing boy was still smiling as he went to help set up the shot. Wardrobe started getting me dressed. My costume was lukewarm and still wet. It felt like the clothes dryer went off too early. Because of the wetness, it was difficult to put my arms into the padding. My skin kept sticking. Wardrobe had tried talcum powder but when it was wet like that, the talcum powder turned into a sticky paste. I just had to push through. Once my outfit was on, wardrobe zipped up my back and I trudged over to the set to see what they had in store for me.

I watched as the art department dressed the set and the tree that I was going to be sitting in. The crew was attaching a large Ewok rope that was held in place next to the tree. Production came over and told me I would cut the little rope that held the big rope in place. I asked them how I was going to cut the rope and the prop department produced an Ewok ax. They handed it to me and it felt heavy. It was no prop. It was a real ax. I would have to balance not only myself on the branch but the weight of the swinging ax. This would be a new challenge.

The crew finished their final touches and I climbed into the bucket of the cherry picker with my stunt buddy, wardrobe, props, and the operator. Up we went. It didn't seem as high but it was still forty feet in the air. I guess I was getting used to it. Still, if I fell, I was dead.

Through the walkie-talkie, I heard production go over what I was to do. We only had one rope for the stunt so we all hoped it would only need one take. Talk about pressure. As I put my head on, I thought of how I was going to get the G-force to be able to get the ax up to speed to cut the rope and not fall off the branch. Oh well, it was time to stop thinking and start doing. I climbed out and got on the branch. I crawled like a dog twirling in a circle before plopping down comfortably. I stood up, turned around, and sat down again, all while balancing on the branch.

Props handed me the ax and away they went, down in the bucket of the cherry picker. All alone in the tree I got a grip on the ax. I held it in one hand and felt for the rope that I had to cut. As I discovered the geography of my little set, I tried to practice my action. This was really the first time. Balanced on the branch, holding on to it with my butt cheeks, was not the ideal lumberjack way of chopping. It was Kevin Thompson's style. I gave the ax a practice swing.

Okay. I gave production a hearty thumb-up. "Action," was called and I got into my swing. I was sure they wanted this action with one chop. I decided to swing for the fence. I hit the rope with a mighty swing and . . . it didn't cut. I swung again. It was still there. It was getting ridiculous. A third time I swang. Finally, I cut through the rope. Sheesh, that was harder than I thought it would be.

"Cut!" I jumped into the cherry picker. Wardrobe removed my head. My stunt buddy was there smiling at me holding up three fingers, making sure it was noted that it took me three tries to cut the rope. I just stared at him. With testosterone flowing I could either hit him or blame it on something else. I didn't have to. The prop guy realized that the ax blade was safety dull, meaning that most movie prop weapons are dulled for safety. He decided that he would sharpen it for the next take. My stunt buddy was still holding up three fingers.

Surprisingly, production was happy with the take. They liked my anxiety of furiously trying to cut the rope. That stupid dull ax! They all started imitating me. I smiled and saw my stunt buddy in the back still holding up three fingers.

I asked if I was needed for the next shot and production said, "no." A jeep skidded to a stop about ten feet from me and Chris jumped out. He would be in the next shot. We tapped each other out as if we are a tag team wrestling duo.

Props were dressing another tree with a similar rope. Production told Chris what they wanted in the scene and he nodded. He was a man of few words. He got dressed and hopped in the cherry picker. Up they went. With a few last-minute details from different crewmembers, he was helped onto the branch, which he straddled with his legs. I wished I had thought of that. I sat on the branch sidesaddle. Props handed him the ax, which looked really familiar. It was the same ax I had used. "Action," was called and with one mighty blow Chris cut the rope. Figured.

My stunt buddy looked down at me. That time he held up one

finger. I yelled at him, "Props sharpened the ax!" He feigned that he couldn't hear me. I knew props sharpened that ax. Production asked props if they have any other prop horns for Chris to blow, but they were back down on the ground. Production was disappointed and told Chris to wave like he was signaling.

Production was happy with Chris's performance. The cherry picker lowered back down to the ground. My stunt buddy caught my eye with his single digit of a finger waving at me. I knew they sharpened that ax. He knew it was getting to me. I had to let it go or he was going to love giving me a hard time. So, I decided to change my attitude.

I congratulated Chris on a job well done. Loudly. I went over the top. I slapped him on the back and shook his hand, all the time saying, "good job!" and "way to go, dude!"

My stunt buddy was speechless. He didn't know what to say. Point for the Ewok stunt guys! I had realized what he was trying to do and turned it around as a team win for us Ewoks. Yes! It was fun to give the guys a good razz. I did it all the time. If I was going to give it, I had to be able to take it. I turned it around on the stormtrooper stunt guy that time. He would be after me again the next time. It made things fun.

Production declared it a wrap on the trees for that day. Chris and I, along with some of the crew, headed out to the next location. Where? I didn't know. And I didn't ask. We would simply drive until we got there, I had learned. I rode with my costume around my waist. I held my pads like a football player holding his shoulder pads. The wind from the open-air jeep felt good against my skin. I enjoyed it, knowing it would be temporary.

# Chapter Forty-One
# Cutting Room Floor

OUR JEEP DROVE up on a scene already in progress. Our driver cut the engine and we watched as they tried to complete it. I had been in so many scenes that I had forgotten how crazy everything could get just trying to get a scene done. It was kind of fun to have a moment to stand on the outside and watch the chaos rather than be a part of it on the inside, performing.

This scene involved a stormtrooper shooting at four running Ewoks. The Ewoks used a tree stump as a battering ram, taking out the stormtrooper. Production thought it would only be two takes before they'd be able to move on. I thought we would be there a while.

The Ewoks had been rehearsing their run up to the stunt storm-trooper and were a little lopsided. They weren't quite in a drill team formation with the footwork. Felix, one of the littler Ewoks, had had it and sat down. Chris and I jumped out of the jeep to help. Chris was chosen so I went to sit down with Felix to watch the show. I was really excited to watch. Chris was now trying to get the guys in a uniform marching pattern. Felix, who was just a little shorter than the other three, had made the group like a table with one leg too short. With Chris, at least they were all level. They had rehearsed and were all ready to suit up. The prop log was placed on their shoulders and… "Action!"

The guy leading the charge tripped over his feet and all four went tumbling into the dirt. We heard a loud, "Oof!"

Nobody was hurt but everybody was busting up. Hearing that voice, come out of an Ewok, was pretty funny. It broke the tension that had started to permeate the set. By take two, they got their footwork together but missed their target and ran by the intended stormtrooper, running into the bushes. For take three, again footwork troubles. Felix and I couldn't help but crack up, mainly because up until that point, *we* had been the ones having all the problems. Take four; the feet didn't fail the boys. Their aim was true and they managed a direct hit on the stunt stormtrooper. Production wanted one more take but then they had to do even a few more because of technical difficulties. When they finally got another good take, the scene wrapped. Just another day on Endor... too bad it didn't make it into the movie!

Another fun scene that didn't make it into the movie was one that involved me, a stunt stormtrooper, and Felix. The stormtrooper was searching the lower brush for hidden Ewoks. As different Ewoks ran from the stormtroopers, one of the stunt guys caught me, lifted me over his head, and threw me. As he did this, Felix swung in from off camera and smacked the stormtrooper with a club, knocking him to the ground. He got back up, looking a little dazed and confused. Felix came swinging back in and clobbered him again. Down he went again.

We had worked it out beforehand by seeing how far my stunt buddy could throw me. Then we set the crash pad accordingly, kind of like throwing a sack of potatoes into a truck. We put Felix in a harness and attached him to a rope upside down. We placed him off camera. When it was go time the extra Ewoks scurried out of their hiding spots as the stunt guy came upon them. Felix, after a few misses, hit him square on the helmet. He then hit him again. The camera crew was cracking up so much; they wanted us to do it again. But the thing was, the stunt guy was getting tired. I didn't blame him. Throwing me wasn't easy. I would be tired, too. I'm heavy. Not to mention the fact that he was also getting whacked with a club. Though it was a prop, the hit still rattled the head a bit. Every take he had to pick me up and throw me. Up and down, up and down. I did mention that I wasn't the lightest thing in the forest.

I was in a few other scenes that were left on the cutting room floor.

There was one that involved me and another Ewok running. We were always running. It was never a nice stroll in the woods. A stormtrooper shot his blaster at us. We ran in our full costumes, minus the heads. The camera set its shot right behind the stormtrooper to give his point of view of us running by him.

We were about to get killed by the stormtrooper. The director yelled, "Bang!" twice, and we went down. I made sure my landing area was free of rocks and branches. We rehearsed a few times and then went back to finish getting dressed.

Special effects were working on our heads. They were putting squibs--small explosives--on the side of my head. I thought, *Cool.* Then I blurted, "Wait, what? You are putting an explosive next to my head?"

The special effects team assured me it was safe. The explosion would go away from my body. I thought back to high school chemistry; fire is hottest at the tip of the flame. There was no boom, just a small flash to show a laser hit. The effects guys put a metal plate on the inside of our heads, just above our left temples. They cut a small hole in the fur to place the squib. The metal plate was to protect us from getting burned by the flash. A wire cord was then threaded under our costumes to our gloved hands. On the end, was a small button. At one precise moment, we could detonate our own squibs. I had an explosion on my head that I was going to detonate myself. That was nuts. Instead of freaking out about it, I thought back to playing in my backyard. This was just one of those dramatic dying scenes I had perfected . . . except now we had live ammo!

I was dressed and ready to explode when I took my starting place. I would be getting shot first. All departments were ready and "Action," was called. We started running. I heard the sound of my stunt buddy's blaster shot and I detonated myself. My head and body recoiled as the squib went off. I hit the ground. I was lucky it was a soft patch. "Cut!"

The crew came over and helped me with my head. Everything had worked fine. Production just wanted to do a few more to get the timing right for the hit. We did it a few more times and it went off without a hitch. I guess that scene didn't make it into the movie because everyone knows a stormtrooper could never hit a moving target.

Another scene that I did that didn't make it into the film was a scene of the Rebels, or it may have been the stormtroopers, running past a burning log with lots of dead Ewoks on the ground. It was a scene of carnage. Extra Ewoks were placed a safe distance from the fire, told not to move. I think everyone liked that. No one had to run. The stunt Ewoks were placed just a little closer to the fire. Production wanted me to be even closer to the log that was on fire. So, I scooted closer. They said, "Even closer." So, I scooted closer. I could now feel the heat from the fire. They said, "Even closer still, Kev, you're still too far."

I crawled on my stomach even closer to the fire. I could really feel the heat now. I smelled something burning and realized… it was me. My costume, I believed, was on fire.

A fireman rushed over and sprayed me with a fire extinguisher, putting out the flames. I could barely breathe because of the restrictive air passage of my head, the smoke from the fire, and now the $CO_2$ fire extinguisher all over the place. I was no longer on fire, but I was having a hard time breathing. Wardrobe came over and took off my head.

The special effects guys controlled the fire. They had regulated propane gas tanks attached to a long hose. The hose was then attached to a metal pipe with holes in it. Then it was placed next to the log. It looked like a log lighter found in many home fireplaces. When the gas was turned on, special effects lit the other end, a real fake fire. We had real firemen standing by just in case something went wrong. Good thing they were there to put me out. My body didn't actually catch on fire. But my Ewok fur had melted. Thank goodness all the costumes had been treated with a fire retardant.

Even though these scenes didn't make it into the final cut, they're fond memories that I cherish. In a way, they have a special place in my heart, probably because they're not in the film for the world to see. My friends and I still talk about shooting them often, reliving the moments and cracking up like kids.

# Chapter Forty-Two
## A Man's Man

O NE PARTICULAR DAY stands out in my mind . . . there was an extra air of excitement. Harrison Ford was coming back to the location to be in a scene where we blew up the bunker. It was the epic explosion where Han Solo removes the invisible shields of the Death Star. The bunker, controlled by the Empire, was where the shields were produced. No scenes were shot inside the bunker building. It was a façade, meaning it was just an outside shell. But it was strong enough that over twenty of us could stand, jump, and run on it. That was where our battle started. That was now where it would end. In a big ball of flame, Han would blow up the bunker. That was what everybody was excited about. It was our 4th of July.

With all the preparations going on, lunchtime was a big deal that day. Everyone wanted to be at the popular table with Harrison and the above the line people. It's funny the way people in show business talk about "above the line" and "below the line." Here we are trying to get rid of labeling and much of the entertainment industry takes pride with equality, but it really is a thing. "Above the line" production describes the executives and stars that have their credits listed before the title of the film. "Below the line" is for those whose credits are listed at the end of the film.

Anyway, that day was especially like middle school again. Everyone scrambled to sit by Harrison. You could instantly tell he was a lowkey, quiet guy who didn't want people scrambling to sit by him. But oh, well. I'm sure he was used to it. I wasn't fast enough, so I didn't make it to the popular table. But I did enjoy watching from the nerd table. I could tell the nearest Ewok was telling Harrison his life story. Everyone around Harrison was trying to play it cool while talking his ear off. Harrison was just trying to eat.

After lunch we went to find the special effects guys rigging the explosives. Everyone searched for somewhere to be—we all wanted the best seat to watch the show. Production wanted everyone at a safe distance so that no one got hurt. I was talking with one of the special effects guys and he gave me a tip on a good spot to watch from. It was up on a hill about one hundred yards away. I was about to make my way over there when J.R. stopped me. He told me to get dressed because he had an idea for a shot. It seemed I would have to watch the scene later in the theatre with my big bowl of popcorn.

Felix, Chris, Michael and I all got dressed. We all wanted to watch, but now we were in the shot. I got dressed up to my neck and the wardrobe ladies handed me my head. I held it in my hand as if it were an army helmet. We leaped out of the wardrobe trailer and jumped into the waiting jeeps. They buzzed up the hill where I had been heading to watch the explosion. I was where I wanted to be, just not able to watch the show.

As the crew set up the camera angle, we started rehearsing. We were to run up the hill, past the camera while the explosion was behind us. J.R. was smart; he realized since we had so many cameras, he could hijack one for a different shot to possibly put in the battle scene. We had to time the shot with the explosion. We would only get one try. So, if something went wrong, it would be no good.

We kept rehearsing the scene until we all knew we were ready. I was first in the lineup followed by Chris, Felix, and Michael. We sat and waited for the explosives. We didn't have to wait long. We hurried, dressed, and lined up. I don't think the crew on the set of the explosion knew what we were doing so we had to just go on our own.

Over the radio we heard the call, "Roll cameras." J.R. had figured out how long it would take before the explosion was detonated. Our camera started rolling. I was not nervous but I was feeling anxious about the explosion. I was told many times that it was going to be big. J.R. yelled "Action," and I started my run. We burst through some bushes that I didn't know were placed in our path. I didn't fall down and I had hoped everyone else following had made it through, too.

I heard a huge *BOOM!* The bunker had been blown. I not only *heard* the deafening blast but I *felt* the sound waves pulse through my body. Even with the thick padding, I felt the shock of it. It almost knocked me down. We ran by the camera and were stopped. I had been counting my steps and knew I was past the camera set up. The other guys ran into me but didn't knock me over.

We removed our heads and took in the big smile on J.R.'s face. I knew then we got the shot he wanted. I realized now why J.R. had been so tough on me. He believed in me, but didn't want me to get too confident, too comfortable, or too cocky. He wanted me to keep pushing myself to be my best. He was like a father to all of us and he didn't want us to get hurt. He looked after us. I appreciated that in him. I grew up fast while working on this movie.

# Chapter Forty-Three
## Bittersweet

THE LAST DAYS of the epic shoot in the Endor forest came up rather quickly. Many of the others—cast and crew—were finishing up and had started saying their goodbyes. I was hearing we would continue filming into the next week. Once a rumor starts, it can spread like wildfire. The bus ride to the set was filled with an unknown excitement because we didn't know if that day was truly our last, but all the signs pointed to it.

We had our breakfast. We dressed in our baby blue pajamas. I was in the first scene, which was another running scene. We didn't wear the stunt outfits that we liked. We dressed in the regular pads. We rehearsed and shot several different set ups of the Ewoks running away from the camera. We shot scenes of Ewoks running toward the camera. I wondered what else we could shoot and who started the rumor that we still had so much to shoot?

During a break in between set ups, I noticed some of the crew putting up a series of wires and cables that were about twenty feet high in the trees. I wondered if this was a stunt I might get to do. It looked like a zip line. I asked one of the crewmembers what it was and he told me that they were going to attach a camera to the wires. Then the Ewoks would run down below. I realized this wasn't a stunt for me or any of the Ewoks. It was a stunt for one of our cameramen!

We waited as the crew set it all up and made sure it was safe. Then the camera department started talking about who was going to be the camera operator. The grip and special effects team were discussing that it had to be a small person because the weight of the rig, the camera, and the operator would all have to be taken into consideration. Someone made a joke about putting Felix up there. It was a good laugh but back to reality. All the operators were too heavy. An assistant cameraman who was in charge of the focus and the lenses, was elected. He had been an assistant for a long time and was ready for the promotion. This was quite an honor for him, similar to how I moved up the ranks of the stunt Ewoks. I felt happy for him.

We rehearsed without the actual camera on the rig as it went down the zip line. A couple of crewmembers ran with cables attached to the rig simulating either the view of an Imperial walker or a speeder bike. I think it was a walker but they didn't stop every four seconds. Once they started running, they didn't stop. After a few rehearsals, we all had our timing right. We suited up.

The cameraman was off getting attached to the rig. I started getting my gloves and head on. I could feel my stunt feet rubbing my own feet raw. The band-aids that covered my blisters had fallen off like they always did. They just wouldn't stick to sweaty bodies. I put my head on and got into position. There would be explosions going off but no one was to be killed in the shot. Everyone was to keep running. I realized what it was—a high angle shot from above covering the whole battle. Michael was in front of me, Felix and Chris were behind me. "Action," was called and we started running.

The pain of the shoes went away as the adrenaline ran through my veins. Explosions were going off all around us. All I could see were flashes of lights. I was counting in my head, like I always did, to remember the landmarks of the forest. I heard the camera rig go whizzing by and I knew I was off camera but I kept running until I heard the director yell, "Cut!" We all stopped without running into each other. The wardrobe ladies came over and took off our heads.

Peter the director then yelled, "That is a wrap on the Endor forest!"

It took me a moment before I realized it was over. Just like that! Wait . . . aren't you going to say, "Cut, perfect, let's go one more time?"

It was really over. We didn't have any more to shoot. I didn't need to put this sweaty costume on. No more twigs in my underwear. No more eating dirt. No more gasping for water. Was I already missing it? A crewmember came over and shook my hand. He gave me a friendly hug. Then he was off. I looked around. Everyone was hugging. The whole crew had gathered around to give each other hugs and cheers of a job well done.

The guys and I were still in our Ewok suits, with our heads off. Everyone was whooping it up. Felix came up to me and shook my hand. He told me I had done a good job. I grabbed him and gave him a big hug. J.R. came up behind us and slapped us on our backs. He had a big smile and he nodded approvingly to both of us. I thanked him for believing in me. He told me that I did a great job and he was proud of me. We talked and joked as we headed to our dressing rooms.

As I got out of my Ewok costume for the last time, I wondered if I would ever wear it again. I was glad to get out of the costume but sad that it was over. I thanked my wardrobe ladies who had dressed and undressed me for so many weeks. They were my unsung heroes.

I had made a lot of friends. I would see most of the Little People actors and extras back in Hollywood. I called many of them friends before the picture and we are still friends today. The English actors, well I didn't know if I would ever see them again. I hoped I would. I hoped I would see everyone again someday. On a film, it is like a family during the holidays. Everyone has a place at the table. Some are setting the table, preparing the side dish or carving the turkey. Everyone is glad to be there but they all want to get out before it's time to do the dishes or Uncle Dale has too much to drink. Even though I wanted to get home, I didn't want to leave because I knew I'd miss being with everyone. It was a weird conundrum. We were all glad to be there. We all wanted to get home to our families but after we left, we wished we were back in the forest.

As we boarded our yellow school bus back to the motel, we were all handed a *Revenge of the Jedi* sweatshirt. We had ordered them earlier and they had finally arrived. It was like the last day of school as we took our final trip up the logging road. We bounced, skidded, and jerked for one more time up the hill. The school bus maneuvered the tight 45-degree turns not quite like a sports car does—but Tommy kept us safe.

I looked out the window as melancholy thoughts rushed in. *Would I miss my Ewok costume?* I thought back to when I was a child playing army in my backyard . . . I thought about how much I had grown on my filming adventure, the friends I had made, and the disagreements that brought us closer together. The Ewok team had grown together. We all went through some very tough times and made it out in one piece.

I realized how fortunate I was to have nailed the audition. I felt so lucky that I had been picked to be a stuntman. I believed our stunt team performed to the best of our abilities—especially given the restrictiveness of the costume. In fact, in my opinion, we performed above and beyond what any other group of actors and extras blended together could have done. Would it be the last time I would view the forest moon of Endor? I was staring out the window watching the abundance of trees whizzing by when Felix startled me, poking me in the ribs from behind. I think I jumped two feet in the air off the bus seat. He looked at me and cracked up. He got me good.

Felix and I talked about the job, life, and about the upcoming party planned for that night. He was feeling the same way. He missed his wife and children and was glad to be going home, but part of him also wanted to keep working. I was not alone in my thoughts. Our yellow school bus rumbled into the motel parking lot for the last time. It was time to party.

# Chapter Forty-Four
## Party Time

I DIDN'T PACK ANY really nice clothes. All I had were some clean jeans and a long-sleeved collared shirt. It would have to do. We were leaving bright and early the next morning so I had to pack that evening, before leaving for the party. Being that I left my car keys in London oh so many months ago I, scavenged my room for any lost socks. I was not going to leave anything behind. I was ready for the trip home.

The party was held across the street at the restaurant/bar. It was the best place in town and basically the only place in town that could hold the cast and crew. Production provided a big bus to get people to and from the party. This was not our yellow school bus. This was a big commuter bus. We were the first ones picked up, and then the bus made more stops on the way to the party, picking up everyone from the various hotels and motels.

We were first on and the designated welcome committee. We continued picking up more partygoers until the bus was full. Every time we would stop and someone would get on, we all raised a good-hearted ruckus trying to embarrass each person like some kind of initiation. We were all one big family.

The party was a lot of fun. It was great to see everyone one last time. It was tough to recognize a lot of people because I was used to seeing them all grimy and dirty. Everyone cleaned up so nice. The music was provided by a local band and at one-point, Kenny Baker got up on stage and played *Mack the Knife* on his harmonica. People were feeling good, eating, drinking, and dancing. A few romances had blossomed. The wardrobe ladies were there with their significant others. It was nice to see them outside of work and finally get to meet their partners. This was their first Hollywood party.

None of the main cast members were there except for Kenny Baker. The party was mainly for the Ewoks, stunt guys, and planet Endor crew. It was more like a family get together than a Hollywood party. At one-point Peter, our director, called for quiet. The band stopped and someone handed Peter the microphone. He grabbed a chair, sat down in the middle of the dance floor, and professed his thanks to all of us. Then he was handed a big sack, as if he was Santa Claus. Peter took out rolled pieces of paper that looked like small diplomas. He called every Ewok by name, one by one and handed us each a certificate that was hand calligraphed on parchment paper.

Peter had something comical to say about each of us. I think he ad libbed his whole speech. The room was having a rollicking good time. People from the crowd would shout out additions to each description, which was a lot of fun. Everyone was laughing. When he came to my name, he said something like, "We tried to kill you many times but you just kept coming back." I didn't realize it at the time, but those certificates were our validation that we were in the movie. Because we are unrecognizable, many people later claimed that they were in the movie. The certificates were our proof.

When the party ended, we boarded the bus. I entered my motel room for the last time and went to bed, all packed up. I woke the next morning to a knock on the door. The bus was there to take us to the airport. I had overslept! I forgot to turn on my alarm. I was now running around my room realizing how much I had *not* packed. I was throwing everything I could find in my suitcase. No order to it, just get it in there. I stuck some toothpaste in my mouth and gargled with some water. As I zipped up my suitcase, I did a once over to make sure I did not leave anything behind.

I paused only slightly to take one last gaze out my window at the meadow that I never explored. Funny, I wanted to get home but now that it was time leave, I wanted to jump out the window and do some exploring. Someone yelled from outside and my daydream vanished. I spit out my mouthwash, wiped my face on a towel, and took one last look at my room. It had been my home for the last five weeks. Nothing left belonged to me. All my possessions were in my suitcase, even my Ewok certificate. I hoped they didn't lose my luggage. I closed the door and ran to the bus. It was of all things, our yellow school bus with Tommy driving. We all got to say hello and good-bye to our dear friend.

# Chapter Forty-Five
## Lips Zipped

THE RIDE TO the airport was quiet. Most people did not get much sleep. We arrived in Los Angeles and we all hugged and said our good-byes. I would see most of my Ewok friends in the coming weeks at *The Hollywood Shorties* practice and rehearsal with the Michael Dunn Theater. My mom was waiting in the car outside. I threw my bag in the trunk and jumped in the front seat. She kissed me on the cheek and then wiped her red lipstick off with her finger.

She told me to put my seatbelt on and that I needed a haircut. Did she forget she was talking to a stuntman? I smiled and clicked my belt. She mentioned that not much had changed at home since I left. I think I had changed a little. I was a big shot on a big movie. But . . . in reality, that job was over and I needed to find a new job. I guess I no longer *was* a big shot. I was just one of my mom's kids looking for his next big gig.

We talked all the way home about my adventures in a place far, far away. I wanted to tell her everything but I had signed that stupid non-disclosure form. It was good she wasn't a *Star Wars* fan. She didn't ask me about the plot. I just said, "It was a lot of hard work and I'd love to tell you all about it, but I can't." My mom knew quite a few of the Little People who were in the film, so I shared stories of some of them and caught her up on how they were doing.

When I got home it was great to sleep in my own bed and eat some home cooking. I would go out with my hometown friends. They'd ask about where I had been, knowing I had been out of town on a movie. I told them it was called, *Blue Harvest* even though they knew I was working on *Revenge of the Jedi*. I winked at them but never uttered the words. They tried to pry details out of me. I only said, "I was an alien." I did not want to spoil the story for them. Was I a bad guy or a good guy? That was for me to know and them to find out. Heck, there was so much to the storyline that *I* didn't even know because I had been stuck on Endor.

There were stories on television, radio, and in newspapers about *Revenge of the Jedi*. It flooded the airways. There was an electric energy in the air surrounding the opening of the movie. I was very excited. I had worked on several films but never on one of that magnitude. Nothing matched the hype that there was for this project. I wondered if I should buy a *Revenge of the Jedi* poster. I kept procrastinating that I would buy it tomorrow. Tomorrow came and the news hit that George Lucas was changing the name from *Revenge of the Jedi* to *Return of the Jedi*. Nuts! I knew I should have bought that poster when I had the chance. The price skyrocketed and the hype of the movie grew even larger.

I was bursting at the seams. I so wanted to tell my friends and family. I could only talk about the movie with my fellow Ewoks. Lucky for me there were quite a few that lived close by. It would only be behind closed doors, never in public, when we would talk about our adventures. We would make sure the windows were closed and the doors were shut. That dang non-disclosure form weighed heavy on all of us. It felt good to be able to swap stories of our times in the redwoods. We were all wondering and waiting if we were actually in the film. Most actors say, "My best scenes are on the cutting room floor." Sure, I would say that too so that no one truly knew if it was your best performance or not. No one wanted to brag about something they had been cut out of. George Lucas, for all we knew, could have gone back and changed the whole scene. Maybe none of us were in it. It was nerve wracking.

I received my package of sweatshirts in the mail and put them under the bed. They were my Christmas gifts for my family. Now that they said *Revenge of the Jedi*, they were very valuable. I had met a girl named Tracey who was very special to me. In fact, I was falling in love with her. I was going to give her one as her Christmas gift. I wondered if she would realize that this was not just any old sweatshirt. This was a real special girl.

When Tracey opened the package, she treasured it. I know because she still has it in our closet. That's right—Tracey's my wife. She was the only one I could tell, other than my fellow Ewoks.

# Chapter Forty-Six
## Starry Eyed

STORYLINES SLIPPED OUT and pictures of Ewoks started appearing in *Return of the Jedi* stories in the press. The only Ewok shown in the promotional images was Warwick's character. We, as a group, still didn't know how much the Ewoks would be seen in the final cut. We'd have to wait for the screening.

When I received my premier pass for the cast and crew screening, I was more than ready to find out. It wouldn't be a big Hollywood screening with the press and paparazzi. Sure, I was a little bummed that I didn't get to go to the big flashy screening, but it was okay. I wanted to see this film so badly it didn't matter! It was in the Darrel F. Zanuck Theater on the back lot of 20th Century Fox Studios. I had my date. She had my sweatshirt and my heart.

One of the best things about going to the screening was getting to see a lot of the people who worked on the movie that I hadn't seen since shooting ended. Even though it was on the back lot, we got dressed up. I not only saw all my Ewok friends, but many of the stormtrooper stunt guys were there as well. We were all slapping hands and swapping stories. Some of the film crew was there too, but sadly, none of the English cast and crew were.

Everyone looked so different, all dressed up. We found a seat with some of our friends and the theater lights dimmed.

Oh, I had been waiting for this.

I was a kid at a Saturday matinee, only this time I was going to be watching myself achieving my dream. My eyes and ears were glued to the screen and I was holding hands with the girl of my dreams.

As I watched our Endor scenes of the Ewok battle I realized I was in almost all of them. George had kept almost all of my scenes! I was swinging, jumping, running, slipping and sliding. There was a reason wardrobe changed my head so many times - it would have looked like the same Ewok was everywhere. I suppose this was what Peter meant when he said, "I was killed many times, but kept coming back." I was all over the film! I knew which Ewoks were me because I lived it.

The audience cheered for the Rebels and booed the Empire. By the end of the movie I was satisfied in every way. The film delivered and our Ewok battle scenes looked amazing. This was the first time any of us had seen our work and we were all very proud.

As the credits rolled, we excitedly looked for our names. The production decided to list the Ewoks alphabetically. The six of us who were contracted as stuntmen were not given credit on the screen as stuntmen. Instead, we were grouped along with the other Ewoks. The other stunt actors *did* get credited. Only us Ewok stunt actors did not. In that moment, it felt like us Little People were underappreciated and overlooked. I can't say it was a new feeling for me, but I was genuinely disappointed. We had worked really hard. We had longer hours as stuntmen and earned our bruises. We were on contract with a higher salary and I was proud to say we made the Ewoks look good by working together, as a team. I had to shift my perspective. Regardless of not receiving an onscreen stunt credit, we knew we had done great work. I had to focus on that and not dwell.

When the lights came up, we all cheered. I walked out of the theater hand in hand with my future wife. I had a skip in my step and my head in the clouds. I could now let everyone know I was in *Return of the Jedi*. I burned that non-disclosure form!

# Chapter Forty-Seven
## Life After Endor and
## the Return of the Costume

ALMOST SIX MONTHS after the premiere of *Return of the Jedi* I was called for an exclusive audition for two made-for-TV movies: *Ewok Adventure* and *Battle for Endor*. The auditions were much more relaxed because I had already proved myself with the work I had done on *Return of the Jedi*.

During the audition I created a character on the fly. I thought about Santa Claus as a tough, strong warrior who was still jovial. The movie was intended for kids and George Lucas wanted to make the film for his daughter, Amanda. It would be released for Thanksgiving, 1984.

Some of the actors from *Return of the Jedi* stole their Ewok costumes on the last day of shooting. They were not called back because they had no costume in storage for them. If only they had known…!

I had some mixed feelings getting back into that costume. I was happy to have the job and honestly was surprised to see I'd be wearing that thing again! I thought those days were behind me! Only this time my costume was more decorated with bones, feathers, and breastplate. I even had my own personal ax. Guess I really wowed 'em with that dull ax bit! My character's name was Chukha-Trok and he was my alter ego warrior. I had my game face on and ready to conquer.

And guess what? This time around I got my own trailer with my name on it! "KEVIN THOMPSON." That felt really good.

I was excited to play Chukha-Trok because now I had a distinct personality. I rode a horse, and—spoiler alert—I had my first death scene as an actor! I thought about my death scene (I think every actor does)—*how would I die?* I had the spirit of John Wayne and all the famous cowboys. In my last breath I gave my signature ax to the child star, Mace. He would use this to step up and be the hero he was meant to be.

I heard, "Cut!" And then a few sniffles . . . I knew I had done it. When I took my costume head off, I saw the crew wearing black armbands in honor of Chukha-Trok's passing. They wore them for the rest of the day. My first death scene was a success! Later I was told that I made Amanda cry. She loved Chukha-Trok. And that was me!

# Epilogue

MORE THAN 30 years after my *Star Wars* journey began, my time as an Ewok continues to impact my life. Every audition I go on, there is at least one person in the room who asks me about *Return of the Jedi*. Their face glazes over in that fandom glow as they ask questions and share what the film meant to them. It breaks the ice and changes the feel of the audition, making it a conversation on an equal level.

I have been inducted into the 501ˢᵗ Legion and the Rebel Legion, philanthropical fraternal organizations, all about *Star Wars*. The Rebel Legion's line is "Good guys doing good," and the 501ˢᵗ Legion is "Bad guys doing good." Both groups dress in *Star Wars* costumes and are extremely serious about getting each and every detail right. I'm proud to say I was brought in as an honorary member to both groups in 2019.

Fans at Comic-Cons, celebrations, and special appearances come up to me and say things like, "Ewoks saved me as a kid." They claim it took them away from drama at home and to a much-needed fantasy world. One of the best things about being a part of the *Star Wars* family and connecting with fans is that there are no stares of judgment or gawking because I'm a Little Person. I am looked at for me, Kevin Thompson, an actor and stuntman who performed with intelligence, machismo, and strength. In my mind, they're looking at me for making an Ewok come alive as a warrior. And that makes me so proud.

This costume character that was the beginning of my career, changed my life. It was a job that I worked really hard on to make a mark on my resume and it has been a mark on my heart forever.

# With Gratitude

*Sometimes I amaze myself*
– Han Solo

IT IS INCREDIBLY ridiculous how I thought that I could easily publish my story about my time as an egotistical young man in my 20's. I was wrong and my wife Tracey told me so. She has heard my stories for 38 years. I jotted my memories on paper here and there.... the thing is that is all I had. Little pieces of paper everywhere. In my pockets, in my car, on sticky notes on the refrigerator. She had enough of hearing my story and reading my little pieces of paper. She warned me if I was to go with her to the market we were going to get in and get out without me telling my stories. She would call it "no circus". I was itching when I would see someone wearing a "Star Wars" shirt or a child carrying the little action figures. I was about to explode with excitement as my lips were held tight together ready to tell them "I was an Ewok in Return of the Jedi". She would give me the look "NO". If I opened my mouth, we would be there an hour longer in frozen foods with a crowd and photo ops. It would be a circus!

She finally sat down and we created this book together. My mother told us "If you can wallpaper a bathroom together you know that your marriage is going to make it". Well, we didn't wallpaper but we wrote a book together. I think it tested us and our marriage. We tell the story so differently. Tracey told me "you sound like an arrogant know it all" and she knew I was really scared to death doing the stunts at 22 years old. She toned my arrogance and brought the book the smells, emotions, sweat and laughter to the pages. The arrogance was my shield.

Tracey and I have so much gratitude and love for the people that supported us. We want to thank our Editor and Friend Suzanne Francis. We honestly couldn't have done it without her. As you see she didn't edit this acknowledgement page therefore we sound like we are rambling. But truly, we are forever grateful for Suzanne. We also want to thank our cousin Heather Knowles. She listened to us and read and re read our book several times. She is our professional author on our team. Thank you, Heather!

Thank you to TK Thomas Travis who let us crash the 501st swag party with him. As soon as we met him, we were instant friends. Our world has opened up in so many ways ever since that day. I can name so many special friends from several Garrisons and Legions across the Nation. We are so honored to be included in your circles.

Thank you to Albin Johnson – Founder, 501st Legion. You have an incredible legacy. I am forever indebted to the 501st members. And a thank you to the Rebel Legion. All the support and philanthropy that they do as well is amazing. People need to be more like you Albin! You have so much compassion that fills the room when you are in it.

I have had so many Beta readers and you all know who you are. Believe me, Tracey and I listened to your ideas and thoughts with much gratitude. Thank you so much for taking the time to read and give us your suggestions.

To all our artist friends especially those who gifted us with their interpretation of Chubbray. Our book cover is amazing by our friend and Artist Hiroshi Kanatani. Thank you!

Thank you, Brandon Jackson "Chief Geek" who always has a camera, in his hand and a smile on his face. You catch so many memorable moments. Your personal Angel shines with you.

I can't even begin to express Tracey and my appreciation to all the fans who have reached out to us. They have stood in line for hours just to meet us and hear our stories. They have bought us drinks and dinners. They have assisted us with all our heavy lifting. They have pointed us in the right direction whether it was to find the bathroom or how to get up on the stage. We have made so many lifelong friends from fans for 40 years. We are extremely blessed to have you all in our lives.

To our parents Thomas and Virginia Thompson as well as Charlotte McCoy. And our families. My father Tommy would always say "my son the Ewok" when he would introduce me and my siblings to all his friends. "This is my son the doctor, my son the dentist, my daughter the chiropractor, and my daughters who are teachers and my son the Ewok." Thank you for being our Force and our biggest support. To our Siblings on both sides of our families who shared in our adventures playing along and not killing us. Thank you!

And of course, our son Wyatt. He came along on this journey unknowingly. He sat with David Prowse and chatted with him not knowing that he was talking to the Dark Lord. He got the VIP passes everywhere he went, he dined with R2D2, Chewbacca, Lando Calrissian, Boba Fett, and many more. He is the son of an Ewok. The tides turned when we sat down to this virtual world. He grew up with the brains in technology. He was able to get our book in the right hands to create it virtually. We are grateful for you Wyatt and we are so proud of the man that you are.

To my fellow Ewoks who worked so hard to make the magic come alive. Be proud of your work, it wasn't easy.

Where would my indigenous tribe be without Mr. George Lucas? Thank you, George Lucas. You have made my life an incredible ride.

To all our friends, families, cast and crew in this galaxy and the ones far far away. May you always know that the Force is with you! We hope to see you soon.

Kevin and Tracey Thompson

# Photos

Me as a baby (far right) with Duke and my siblings.

Family home with the wrap around veranda

Me at 12 years old playing starting 2ⁿᵈ baseman on
The Hollywood Shorties Baseball Team

The World's Smallest Professional Baseball and Basketball Team.
Courtesy photo: Ryan Green

Kevin Thompson

My 1980's Headshot that got me the job on Return of the Jedi

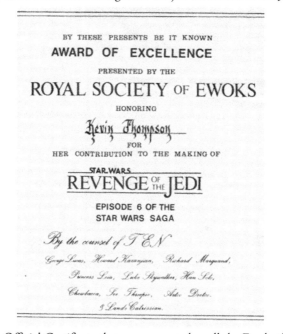

BY THESE PRESENTS BE IT KNOWN

AWARD OF EXCELLENCE

PRESENTED BY THE

ROYAL SOCIETY OF EWOKS

HONORING

*Kevin Thompson*

FOR

HER CONTRIBUTION TO THE MAKING OF

STAR WARS

REVENGE OF THE JEDI

EPISODE 6 OF THE
STAR WARS SAGA

*By the counsel of TEN*

George Lucas, Howard Kazanjian, Richard Marquand,
Princess Leia, Luke Skywalker, Han Solo,
Chewbacca, See Threepio, Artoo Deetoo.
& Lando Calrissian.

My Official Certificate that was presented to all the Ewoks that
worked on "Revenge" of the Jedi. I am proud of this!

**BLUE HARVEST**

| Picture | Shooting Call | Producer | Date |
|---|---|---|---|
| BLUE HARVEST | 8A | H Kazanjian | Saturday, May 8, 1982 |
| LEAVE HOTEL: | 7A | | Director R Marquand |
| LOCATION: Crescent City, Calif. | | | |

| SC. NO. | SET DESCRIPTION | D/N | PAGES | LOCATION |
|---|---|---|---|---|
| 115pt. 119pt. | EXT. FOREST | D | 2 1/8 | BUNKER |
| 124  131 | (Cast #'s: 2,3,5,6,7,8,9,10,11, | | | |
| | STNTS, ATMOS) | | | |
| | The Battle - Conclusion (to complete) | | | |
| | (Storybrd.#'s: 1,2,3,4,5,19,20,21,37, | | | |
| | 38,39,41,36,42,44,45) | | | |

### ADVANCE

| Day/Date | Scenes | pages | location |
|---|---|---|---|
| Sunday, May 9 | First Unit Travel/Second Unit Rest | | |
| Monday, May 10 | T.B.A. | | |

NOTE: The entire company-cast and crew alike-should be aware that the SET IS CLOSED. No visitors! No husbands, wives, children or friends will be allowed to visit the set.

Conditions:     Cover Set:

| Cast and Bits | Part Of | Lv. Hotel | Makeup | On Set | NO. | Crew | Hotel | Lv. Hotel |
|---|---|---|---|---|---|---|---|---|
| Martin | | HOLD | | | 1 | Director | | 7AM |
| Caroline | | 6:30AM | 7AM | 8AM | 1 | Unit Spvsr-M.Herman | | O/C |
| Harry | | 7AM | 7:30AM | 8AM | 2 | Cameraman | | 7AM |
| William | | HOLD | | | 1 | Cameraman  ILM | | |
| Anthony | | 7AM | 7:30AM | 8AM | 1 | 1st Asst. Dir. | | |
| Peter | | ↓ | ↓ | ↓ | 1 | Art Dir. | | |
| Kenny | Wicket | 7AM | 7:30AM | 8:30AM | 1 | Production Des. | | |
| J. Purvis | TEEBO | | | | 1 | 2nd Asst. Dir. | | |
| M. Edmonds | LOGRAY | ↓ | ↓ | ↓ | 1 | Script Sup. | | |
| N. Read (M) | NICKY | 9AM | (Go to school) | | 2 | Prod. Asst. | | |
| W. Davis (M) | WARWICK | 9AM | (Go to school) | | 2 | Cam Op | | |
| P. Diamond | SSP | HOLD | | | 2 | Cam. Op  ILM | | |
| D. Beer | | 7AM | 7:30AM | 8AM | 6 | Cam. Assts. | | |
| B. Horrigan | | | | | 2 | Cam Asst ILM | | |
| P. Henson | | | | | 1 | Mixer | | |
| C. Skeaping | | | | | 2 | Sound Crew | | ↓ |
| J. LeFlore | | | | | 1+1 | Stunt Coord | | |
| L. Holt | | | | | 3 | Makeup | | 1@6:30/7 |
| D. Zormeier | | ↓ | | | 5 | Creature Mll | | 7AM |
| T. Eddon | | ↓ | ↓ | ↓ | 1 | Hairdresser | | ↓ |
| Part of Warwick stunt double | | 7AM | 7:30AM | 8AM | 1 | Teacher | | 9AM |
| K. Thompson | | ↓ | | | 19 | Costumers | | 9@6:30AM |
| F. Silla | | ↓ | | | 6 | Gaffers | | 7AM |
| | | | | | 6 | Electricians | | |
| No. | Extras | Report to | on set | | 1 | Key Grips | | |
| 6 | Stand-ins | Saxton's | 7AM | 7:30AM | 6 | Grips | | ↓ |
| 6 | Stormtroopers | | | 8AM | 6 | Prop Crew | | |
| 5 | Scooter troops | | | | 8 | Special FX | | |
| 8 | Controllers | | | | 5 | Greens | | |
| 2 | Officers | | ↓ | ↓ | 1 | Painter | | |
| 12 | Rebel troops | | | | 1 | Gen.Op. | | 6AM |
| 35 | Ewoks | | p.u.@7AM | 8:30AM | 1 | 1st Aid | | ↓ |
| | | | | | X | Construction | | See Dep |
| | | | | | 2 | Craft Service | | 7AM |
| | | | | | 1 | local contact | | O/C |

TRANSPORTATION

Note: All calls per Cptn unless otherwise noted

| | | |
|---|---|---|
| Car | ward  on loc | |
| Car | | |
| Car | Honeywgn  on loc | |
| car | | |
| Bus | | |
| Bus | | |
| Camera-Sound | on loc | |
| Prop | on loc | |
| Grip-Elec. | on loc | |
| Generator | on loc | |
| Utility Trk. | | |
| Set Dress. Trk. | | |
| Constr. Trk. | | |

| Dept. | SPECIAL INSTRUCTIONS: |
|---|---|
| | ALL DEPTS: The viewing of dailies is restricted. Please check with the Production office before attending screening. |
| SP EFX | Walker, Laser hits |
| MU/WRD | Leia wounded |

| No. | Meals | Rdy @ |
|---|---|---|
| X | brkfst | 6AM |
| 300 | lunch | 12:30PM |
| | dinner | |

✱ THIS FILM IS STRICTLY CONFIDENTIAL!
DO NOT DISCUSS YOUR WORK WITH OUTSIDERS.

K. Thompson is me as an official "stuntman".
Notice: Kenny Baker was originally cast as Wicket

190

LOCATION CALL SHEET  Day of Shooting [3] 2ND UNIT

| Picture: | Shooting Call: | Producer: | | Date: |
|---|---|---|---|---|
| BLUE HARVEST | 8AM | H. Kazanjian | | Wednesday, May 12, 1982 |
| LEAVE HOTEL: | 7AM | | | Director: David Tomblin |
| LOCATION: | Crescent City, California | | | |

| SC NO | SET DESCRIPTION | D/N | PAGES | LOCATION |
|---|---|---|---|---|
| 124 | EXT. ENDOR FOREST | D | | BUNKER |
| | Han and Chewie run from Bunker | | | |
| | (Complete 1st Unit) | | | |
| 115 | EXT. ENDOR FOREST | D | | BUNKER |
| | Various shots of battle between | | | |
| | Ewoks and Stormtroopers | | | |
| | R2 and 3PO lure Troopers into trap | | | |

ADVANCE

| DAY/DATE | Scenes | Pages | Location |
|---|---|---|---|
| Thurs. May 13 | EXT. ENDOR FOREST - Misc. Battle | | BUNKER |
| Fri. May 14 | EXT. ENDOR FOREST - Misc. Battle | | BUNKER |

NOTE: The entire company-cast and crew alike should be aware that the SET IS CLOSED. No husbands, wives, children and/or friends will be allowed to visit the set. NO VISITORS!

| Cast and Bits | Part Of | Lv. Hotel | Makeup | On Set | No. | Crew | Hotel | Lv. Hotel |
|---|---|---|---|---|---|---|---|---|
| Kenny | Wicket | 7A | 7:30A | 8A | 1 | Director | | 7A |
| J. Purvis | Teebo | | | | 1 | Unit Spvsr. | | O/C |
| M. Edmonds | Logray | ✓ | ✓ | ✓ | 1 | Cameraman | | 7A |
| N. Read (M) | Nicky | 9A | 9:30A | 10A | 1 | Cameraman-ILM | | |
| W. Davis (M) | Warwick | 9A | 9:30A | 10A | 1 | 1st Asst. Dir. | | |
| Felix Silla | | 7A | 7:30A | 8A | 1 | Art Dir. | | |
| Kevin Thompson | | 7A | 7:30A | 8A | 1 | Production Des | | |
| D. Beer | Sep. | 7:30A | 8A | 8:15A | 1 | 2nd. Asst. Dir | | |
| B. Horrigan | | | | | 1 | Script Spvsr. | | |
| C. Skeaping | | | | | 2 | Prod. Asst. | | |
| J. LeFlore | | | | | 2 | Cam Op | | |
| L. Holt | | ✓ | ✓ | ✓ | 2 | Cam Op ILM | | |
| D. Zormeier | | 7A | 7:30A | 8A | 6 | Cam Assts. | | |
| T. Eddon | | 7:30A | 8A | 8:15A | 2 | Cam Asst. ILM | | ✓ |
| Harry | | 7A | 7:30A | 8A | 4 | Fireman | | 6:30A |
| Anthony | | 7A | 7:30A | 8A | 2 | Stnt. Coord. | | 7A |
| | | | | | 3 | Makeup | | |
| | | | | | 7 | Creature MU | | |
| | | | | | 1 | Hairdresser | | ✓ |
| | | | | | 1 | Teacher | | 9A |
| | | | | | 18 | Costumers | | 7A |
| | | | | | 1 | Gaffers | | |
| | | | | | 6 | Electricians | | |
| | | | | | 1 | Key Grip | | |

| No. | Extras | | Report to | On Set | | Crew | | |
|---|---|---|---|---|---|---|---|---|
| 3 | Standins (Robert, Gary, Richard) | Saxton's | 7A | 7:30A | 5 | Grips | | |
| 10 | Stormtroopers ) continuity | | | | 6 | Prop Crew | | |
| 6 | Rebels | | | | 9 | Special Efx | | |
| 29 | Ewoks | Hotel | ✓ | ✓ | 5 | Greens | | |
| | | | | | 1 | Painter | | ✓ |
| | | | | | 1 | Gen. Op. | | 6:30A |
| | | | | | 1 | First Aid | | 6:30A |
| | | | | | | Construction | | See Dept. |
| | | | | | 3 | Craft Service | | 7A |
| | | | | | 1 | Local Contact | | O/C |

TRANSPORTATION

Note: All calls per Cptn unless otherwise noted

| Car | ward on loc | | | | | |
|---|---|---|---|---|---|---|
| Car | | | | | | |
| Car | Honeywgn on loc | | | | | |
| car | | | | | | |
| Bus | | | | | | |
| Bus | | | | | | |
| Camera-Sound | on loc | | | | | |
| Prop | on loc | | No | Meals | Rdy @ | |
| Grip-Elec. | on loc | | X | brkfst | 6:30A | |
| Generator | on loc | | 225 | lunch | 12:30P | |
| Utility Trk. | | | | dinner | | |
| Set Dress. Trk. | | | | | | |
| Constr. Trk. | | | | | | |

| Dept. | SPECIAL INSTRUCTIONS |
|---|---|
| | ALL DEPTS: The viewing of dailies is restricted. Please check with the Production office before attending screening. |
| SFX | Walker, squibs, bunker explosions, wrecked R2, mobile R2 |
| Grip | Stunt platform near Bunker |

* THIS FILM IS STRICTLY CONFIDENTIAL!
DO NOT DISCUSS YOUR WORK WITH OUTSIDERS.

Ewoks and Stormtroopers all day!

Me as Chubbray the signature white face slash.
Courtesy photo: Lydia Green Graber

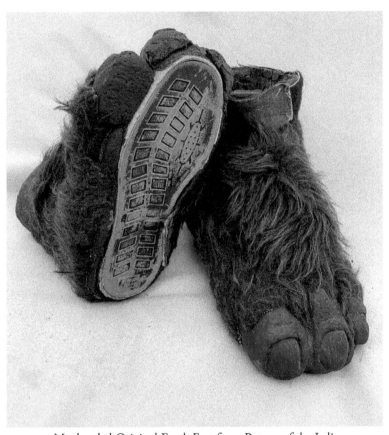

My dreaded Original Ewok Feet from Return of the Jedi.

Redwood tree from my point of view. I climbed many while in my Ewok Costume.

In the shadows and the Fernus Gigantus. The dreaded ferns that would trip us up.

Thunderbird Motel where the Ewoks were housed
during the filming of Return of the Jedi

My Motel Room. Home away from home.

The Ship to Shore where The Production Office was housed.
It is still there shipwrecked.

I am at Celebration Chicago with Tracey and our friends. Thomas TK Travis is on
the far right. Courtesy photo: Brandon Jackson Chief Geek Photography.

Me in the middle with all the Slave Princess Leias at Celebration Chicago
Courtesy photo: Brandon Jackson Chief Geek Photography

Standing beside my alter ego Chubbray.
Created by Andrew Shaddox on the far right

Making friends

Kissing up to the Jedi Master

Signing autographs bring me great joy. Fans become friends.

WonderCon Anaheim, CA. I am having the time of my life after so many years of filming Return of the Jedi. Courtesy photo: Brandon Jackson Chief Geek Photography

My traditional headshot today. No more handstands!